WITHDRAWN

CAMBRIDGE MUSIC HANDBOOKS

Schubert: *Die schöne Müllerin*

CAMBRIDGE MUSIC HANDBOOKS

GENERAL EDITOR Julian Rushton

Cambridge Music Handbooks provide accessible introductions to major musical works, written by the most informed commentators in the field.

With the concert-goer, performer and student in mind, the books present essential information on the historical and musical context, the composition, and the performance and reception history of each work, or group of works, as well as critical discussion of the music.

Other published titles

Schubert: *Die schöne Müllerin*

Susan Youens

Professor of Music,
University of Notre Dame

CAMBRIDGE
UNIVERSITY PRESS

Published by the Press Syndicate of the University of Cambridge
The Pitt Building, Trumpington Street, Cambridge CB2 1RP
40 West 20th Street, New York, NY 10011–4211, USA
10 Stamford Road, Oakleigh, Victoria 3166, Australia

© Cambridge University Press 1992

First published 1992

Printed in Great Britain at the University Press, Cambridge

*A catalogue record for this book
is available from the British Library*

Library of Congress cataloguing in publication data

Youens, Susan.
Schubert, Die schöne Müllerin / Susan Youens.
p.   cm. – (Cambridge music handbooks)
ISBN 0 521 41091 6 (hardback). – ISBN 0 521 42279 5 (paperback)
1. Schubert, Franz, 1797–1828. Schöne Müllerin. I. Title.
II. Series.
ML410.S3Y7 1992
782.42168 – dc20 91–28960 CIP

ISBN 0 521 41091 6 hardback
ISBN 0 521 42279 5 paperback

Contents

Illustrations

The poet of 'Die schöne Müllerin'

It was a fateful encounter for the world of music when Franz Schubert first discovered the poetry of the young Prussian writer Wilhelm Müller (1794–1827), but we do not know when, where, or how. One of Schubert's friends from his schooldays at the Vienna Convikt, Benedikt Randhartinger (1802–93), claimed in later life to have witnessed the discovery and told several versions of his charming but inaccurate tale to Heinrich Kreissle von Hellborn, the composer's first biographer, and others. In the Kreissle version, Schubert at some unspecified time visited Randhartinger at the home of Louis, Count Széchényi of Sárvár-Felsö-Vidék, for whom Randhartinger worked as a private secretary. When the Count called his secretary, Schubert, left to his own devices, found a poetic anthology massively entitled *Seventy-Seven Poems from the Posthumous Papers of a Wandering Horn-Player* by Müller on his friend's desk and took it away, without waiting for Randhartinger to return. When Randhartinger sought him out the next day in order to retrieve his missing book, Schubert begged his pardon and then showed his astonished friend the beginning of the cycle, already composed overnight.[1] However, Randhartinger, increasingly prone in old age to embellish his Schubert anecdotes, did not become secretary to Count Széchényi until 1825, that is, *after* the publication of Schubert's setting of *Die schöne Müllerin* in 1824. In other versions, Schubert visited his friend at Randhartinger's home in the Herrengasse, not at Count Széchényi's, and the number of poems set to music overnight varied from three to seven (*Memoirs*, 200).[2] Although there is no concrete evidence for the supposition, it is also possible that Carl Maria von Weber, to whom Müller dedicated his second anthology of *Waldhornisten* poems in 1824,[3] might have been the intermediary who introduced Schubert to Müller's works, as yet unknown to the Viennese literati, in 1823. Weber came to know Schubert during his visit to Vienna from 17 February to 20 March 1822 and, according to a letter now lost, praised the younger composer's opera *Alfonso und Estrella*, D. 732, warmly.

Who was the poet whose verse so impressed Schubert and many other composers? Many present-day musicians hold the 'simple and naive' Müller in contempt, but literary scholars and a few dissenters from the musical realm have felt otherwise, justifiably so. Müller is neither simple nor naive: he subverts Romantic themes in sophisticated ways, and he adapted the forms of folk poetry to un-folk-like uses. He was famous in his own day and throughout much of the nineteenth century as the 'Greek Müller', one of the foremost German philhellenes who supported the cause of Greek independence from the Ottoman Empire. The young Heinrich Heine wrote to Müller to thank him for demonstrating how a poet could put new wine in the old bottles of folksong forms,[4] and an enthusiastic American proponent of the German poet, Henry Wadsworth Longfellow, praised 'Wohin?' in *Hyperion: A Romance* as typical of Müller's 'pretty songs, in which the momentary, indefinite longings and impulses of the soul of man find expression'.[5] Dated words for dated verse, Müller's detractors might say, but close reading of some – not all – of his verse reveals poetry of a higher order than the legend of 'Müller's mediocrity redeemed by great music' would allow.

The myth of Schubert's supposed lack of literary sensibility has been thoroughly refuted by now. Whether a poem elicited musical ideas was the primary criterion, of course, and he had no qualms about editing poetry for conversion into musical form, but his choices of poetry-for-music reveal a generally discriminating taste. He would on occasion dismiss poetry in blunt terms ('This poem has nothing of music in it', he once told Johann Gabriel Seidl, although he *did* set eleven other poems by Seidl), and he had decided tastes in the matter. The singer to whom Schubert dedicated *Die schöne Müllerin*, Karl Freiherr von Schönstein (1791–1876), writes in his reminiscences of Schubert that the poet Joseph Freiherr von Zedlitz wanted Schubert to set his ballad 'Die nächtliche Heerschau', but the composer refused, 'as he felt he was not in a position to write good music to this poem' (*Memoirs*, 104).[6] In light of those who still condemn Müller as a writer of simple pseudo-folksongs, it is interesting to observe that Schubert had little interest in folk or even folk-like poetry. He must have known the famous anthology *Des Knaben Wunderhorn*, yet neither it, nor any poetry by Clemens Brentano, Achim von Arnim (the compilers and writers of *Des Knaben Wunderhorn*), or Joseph von Eichendorff, appear in his list of texts. He did, however, adopt Müller wholeheartedly.

The poet and his works

Johann Ludwig Wilhelm Müller was born on 15 October 1794 in Dessau, then a provincial town on the river Mulde north of Leipzig.[7] The only surviving child of a poor tailor, Müller's studies in philology, history, and literature at Berlin University in 1812–13 were sponsored by Duke Leopold Friedrich of Anhalt-Dessau, who later gave Müller the post of ducal librarian in 1820 and appointed him *Hofrat* (privy councillor) in 1824. His studies were interrupted after one year by the War of Liberation in 1813, in which Müller fought in the battles of Lützen and at Haynau and Kulm. After his return to Berlin in late 1814, his talent and charm gained him entrée to the city's literary salons, where he met such notable Romantic writers as Friedrich Baron de la Motte Fouqué, Clemens Brentano, and Achim von Arnim. In 1817, his professors, decrying the restless young man's lack of concentration on a single field of study, recommended that he accompany one Baron von Sack on a journey through Greece, Asia Minor, and Egypt. The pair spent two months in Vienna before travelling to Italy, and it was there that Müller's ardent philhellenism was born. It is intriguing to speculate that he might have encountered Schubert during those two months, but there is no evidence for such an occurrence. Although Müller would have preferred a post in Dresden, Berlin, or Leipzig, he settled in his home town after his return from Rome in December 1818 and there began a career as a librarian, teacher, editor, translator, critic, and poet. Despite his constant restlessness (*Wanderlust* is a major theme of his life and his verse), he was happily married from 1821 on to Adelheid von Basedow (1800–83). His good fortune did not last long: he died unexpectedly during the night of 30 September/1 October 1827, just as Schubert was completing the composition of *Winterreise*, D. 911.

Müller's works reflect the interests of many German intellectuals and poets of his day: translations and studies of medieval German literature, folk poetry, novellas, Italian travel lore, Homeric studies, philhellenic poems, and critiques of contemporary English and German poetry – an impressive catalogue for so short a life. Most of Müller's lyric verse was published in the two companion volumes of *Gedichte aus den hinterlassenen Papieren eines reisenden Waldhornisten* (1820 and 1824). The elaborate title is a compendium of Romantic linguistic emblems, even though many of the poems part company with the spirit of Romanticism: wandering, music, horn-calls, humble folk (the *Waldhornist* represents the common people), relics from the past, death, even magic numbers (the 'seventy-seven' poems in the first anthology). The poetry in both collections is grouped in sets and cycles, mostly non-narrative. Both *Die schöne Müllerin* and *Die Winterreise* are exceptions to his usual practice, best exemplified by the lovely cycle *Frühlingskranz aus dem Plauenschen Grunde bei Dresden*, with its unifying theme of spring conquering winter, from the *Waldhornisten-Gedichte II*. The poetic personae of the two anthologies are largely conventional characters from the standard repertoire of shepherds, harvesters, fishermen, apprentices, sailors, maidens in love, millers, hunters, night watchmen, drinkers galore, and, above all, the wanderers endemic in early-nineteenth-century verse, travellers both blessed and cursed, on quests of many kinds.

The gregarious Müller wrote numerous drinking songs, grouped together in the *Tafellieder für Liedertafeln* (Drinking songs for choral societies) printed in the *Waldhornisten-Gedichte II*, and epigrams spiked, like the drinking songs, with acid political commentary – titles such as 'Bad times, good wine' and 'The new demagogue' did not escape the censor's notice. His frequent brushes with the government's powerful censorship bureaucracy began as early as 1816, when he and five friends published a volume of poetry entitled *Die Bundesblüthen* (*Blossoms from the league*) just after the Prussian monarch had forbidden all mention of 'secret societies' in print. Müller, however, was no martyr for his beliefs and, despite bitter complaints to his friend and publisher Friedrich Arnold Brockhaus, often complied with the censors' strictures. *Die schöne Müllerin* (*Im Winter zu lesen*) or *The beautiful miller's daughter* (*To read in wintertime*) would have given government bureaucrats no cause for alarm, but not all of his works were so politically innocuous.

The genesis of the poetic cycle

The history of *Die schöne Müllerin* begins with events in late 1816 – early 1817 and culminates, after Müller's travels in Italy, in the completion of the cycle in 1819–20. Müller became part of a circle of friends who met at the Bauhofstrasse home of the privy councillor Friedrich August von Stägemann (1763–1840), an amateur poet interested in old German traditions. Friedrich August's wife Elisabeth, an accomplished amateur singer and actress and, like her husband, a published poet, brought together a group of brilliant young literary talents for the sake of her son August and her sixteen-year-old daughter Hedwig (1799–1891), the original 'beautiful miller maid'.[8] The younger *Deutsche Gesellschaft* (the Stägemanns also hosted a circle of older artists, E. T. A. Hoffmann and Achim von Arnim among them) included Müller, then twenty-three; the twenty-two-year-old

Wilhelm Hensel (1794–1861), who became a noted portrait artist and Fanny Mendelssohn's husband; his eighteen-year-old sister Luise Hensel (1798–1876), a gifted poet whose children's prayer 'Müde bin ich, geh zur Ruh' (I am weary and go to sleep) is still anthologized in collections of nineteenth-century verse; and the publisher Friedrich Förster (1791–1868), among others. These were the principal players in the poetic tourney that probably began in November of 1816, a game with marked biographical subcurrents. Müller was in love with Luise Hensel, a complex personality whose inner conflicts between *eros* and *caritas* led eventually to her renunciation of marriage and a life devoted to religious charities. Müller's diary for 1815–16 is largely dominated by his love for this young woman. The entry for 8 November 1815 is typical:

Whatever I have done, thought, felt, spoken, or created that is good and beautiful, I have created, spoken, and felt through you. Whatever evil and hateful remains is left over from the time of sensuality and freethinking that held me too long in its chains. Luise, my thanks to you are too great to express: you have saved my soul, my immortal soul. I have you to thank for eternal blessedness – you alone – also perhaps for transitory earthly blessedness as well.

He then re-reads the heated effusion critically and finds it incomprehensible, excessive, and full of clichés but refuses to alter what he has written because his emotion is too great for artistic constraint – a precursor of the miller in 'Pause', who says, 'I cannot sing any more; my heart is too full; I do not know how I can force it into rhyme.' One day, he wrote the question 'Luise, do you love me?' and the words 'Yes' and 'No' on pieces of paper and was playing with them; at first, the answer was 'Yes', but an unlucky rearrangement produced a conjunction of Yes and No: 'Ja, nein Wilhelm' (Yes, [but] not Wilhelm).[9] In this touchingly youthful anecdote is possibly the origin of 'Der Neugierige' and a world that shrinks to the boundaries of two single words. Müller's diary breaks off just before Christmas 1816. Clemens Brentano had met Luise at the Stägemann's house in October, had fallen violently in love with her, and proposed marriage that Christmas. With the advent of the older poet's stormy (and ultimately unsuccessful) suit, Müller's dreams of marrying Luise ended, and so does the diary.

The *Liederspiel*, or a narrative play in verse and song (a cross between a *Singspiel* and a song cycle invented by Johann Friedrich Reichardt as an attempt to reform the *Singspiel*), was a genre performed by professional theatrical companies and by *Liederkreis* societies and artistic salons in the early nineteenth century.[10] For their *Liederspiel*, the young poets of the Stägemann circle chose the venerable tale of a miller maid wooed by various suitors, a subject with numerous models in literature and music. Giovanni Paisiello's comic opera *L'amor contrastato, o sia La bella molinara* of 1788 with its famous air 'Nel cor più non mi sento', had been very popular in Germany and Austria in various German translations, some entitled *Die schöne Müllerin*; it was performed in Vienna in 1822, and Schubert could possibly have heard it the year before he composed his song cycle to a different version of the miller maid's multiple suitors. Another important source for the *Liederspiel* was Goethe's set of four miller-ballads – 'Edelknabe und Müllerin' (The young lord and the miller maid), 'Junggeselle und Mühlbach' (The young journeyman apprentice and the mill-stream), 'Der Müllerin Verrat' (The miller maid's betrayal), and 'Der Müllerin Reue' (The miller maid's remorse) – with their talking brook, journeyman, miller maid, and young aristocrat as the lyric protagonists. 'Junggeselle und Mühlbach' in particular seems to have inspired Müller's creation of a brook-confidante for his miller; Goethe's journeyman miller who bids the brook 'Geh', sag ihr gleich und sag ihr oft' was clearly the model for Müller's 'Eifersucht und Stolz', in which his miller tells the brook 'Geh', Bächlein, hin und sag ihr das'. Given the musical talents of several members of the group, they would probably also have known Reichardt's settings of Goethe's mill poems.[11]

Other sources for the *Liederspiel* came from folk poetry and the various imitations of folk idioms by learned poets. Achim von Arnim and Clemens Brentano's anthology *Des Knaben Wunderhorn* includes a poem entitled 'Der Überlaufer' (The Deserter) in which a maiden named Rose abandons the poetic speaker for a huntsman:

(*3rd and final stanza*)

Hört ihr nicht den Jäger blasen	Do you not hear the huntsman blowing
In dem Wald auf grünem Rasen,	his horn in the green forest,
Den Jäger mit dem grünen Hut,	the hunter with the green hat
Der mein' Schatz verführen tut?[12]	who seduced my sweetheart?

Joseph von Eichendorff's 'In einem kühlen Grunde' (There stands a mill-wheel in a cool riverbank); Clemens Brentano's 'Der Rhein und seine Nebenflüsse' (The Rhine and its tributaries), in which the river Lohre announces 'Von dem Müllerburschen sing ich, / Der sein treue Lieb verlor' (I sing of the miller lad who lost his true love); and Justinus Kerner's eccentric first novel, *Reiseschatten von dem Schattenspieler Luchs* of 1811, with its shy, poetically inclined miller lad outdone by a bold hunter, are other predecessors that the group might have known.[13] Müller, prone to using borrowed themes as springboards for his own imagination, took motifs from Eichendorff for several of his own poems, including 'Der Jäger' in *Die schöne Müllerin* (see ch. 4, p. 56) and 'Die Post' from *Die Winterreise* (the wanderer in that cycle hears a posthorn and his heart leaps, like Eichendorff's poetic persona in 'Sehnsucht' or 'Longing'). The poet Friedrich Rückert, a friend of Müller's in Italy, had written a poem on the miller-maid theme, 'Die Mühle wogt wohl Tag und Nacht' (The mill works both day and night) for his *Jugendlieder* of 1810–13, later published in the *Liebesfrühling*; Müller may have borrowed the motif of frenetic activity to impress the maiden from Rückert's second stanza and improved upon it for his poem 'Am Feierabend'.[14]

For their *Liederspiel* 'Rose, die Müllerin', the Stägemann company assigned roles as follows: Hedwig was Rose the miller maid, and her suitors were Friedrich Förster as a *Junker* or country squire; Müller, predestined by his name, as the journeyman miller; Wilhelm Hensel as the hunter; and Luise Hensel as a gardener. There were other minor roles, possibly including a fisherman, but none of those poems is extant, and the chroniclers cite only the principal parts and players. We know from one of Brentano's letters of December 1816 (he was, speculatively, involved in the venture as a literary advisor) that the *Liederspiel* was acted with whatever gestures and vocal inflections the amateur actors considered appropriate.[15] The play that emerged from their improvisatory efforts has the young miller prevailing briefly over the other suitors – this is not so in the later cycle – and then committing suicide when Rose spurns him for the hunter. Furthermore, in the Stägemann play, the miller is only one of the roles, not the sole story-teller, and the tale continues beyond the point where the later song cycles end. The miller maid, overcome by remorse, subsequently throws herself into the brook as well, after which the others sing songs of mourning for her.[16]

The first song cycle and early versions of the poetry

Some time in November or early December 1816, the group asked Luise to bring her music teacher, the thirty-eight-year-old virtuoso pianist and composer Ludwig Berger (1777–1839), to the house for a performance. Berger, who was also in love with Luise Hensel and proposed marriage to her in February 1817 (?), liked the playlet; according to the poet and music critic Ludwig Rellstab (1799–1860), who published a biography of his deceased friend in 1846, Berger first set Hedwig von Stägemann's 'Wies Vöglein möcht ich ziehen' with its refrain 'Ich habe das Grün so gern' to music.[17] When Berger's setting met with the group's approval, he agreed to set some of the other poems as a song cycle. In Müller's diary for 14 December 1816, Müller writes that he had gone to visit the Hensels and had stayed with Luise 'until seven o'clock, when I went to see Berger, who had requested our presence [Wilhelm Hensel and Müller] for the evening'; one can therefore infer that Berger was already at work on the cycle before Christmas 1816.[18] Five of the poems he chose were Müller's and the young poet was his principal collaborator. Rellstab relates that the composer worked slowly and painfully and that he (Rellstab) was a witness to Berger torturing Müller with demands for revision. The poet supposedly complied gladly, seeing the beautiful musical results. One wonders if Müller was really so amenable, although he could well have been deferring to a musical talent he respected – the virtuoso pianist and well-known composer was far more eminent than the young poet at the time. The collaboration ended when Müller left for Italy in August, and Berger's ten songs were published the following year by the newly-founded firm of E. H. G. Christiani as the *Gesänge aus einem gesellschaftlichen Liederspiele 'Die schöne Müllerin'*, Op. 11. These songs offer a unique glimpse into the world of private salons and the genesis of an emerging art form: the set is a remarkable link between staged dramatic works (these are songs *from* a *Liederspiel*, not a *Liederspiel* itself) and concert lieder cycles, such as Schubert's.

Berger's five Müller settings in his *Die schöne Müllerin* cycle also preserve earlier versions of those poems by a poet given to revision, whatever his occasional assertion of spontaneous inspiration. In his diary, he wrote that 'I often carry a song about with me for a long time; I finish and refine it within, then write it down quickly and without alteration. These are my best pieces.'[19] However, in 1827, he told the Leipzig publisher Friedrich Arnold Brockhaus, 'I am very scrupulous about style and count syllables anxiously',[20] and the habit of tinkering with his poems was evident early. With each stage of publication, he revised and refined the poems born of the Stägemann *Liederspiel*. The variants in Berger's cycle might well reflect, so we are told, the composer's wishes; the same poems appear in contemporary literary periodicals with details altered from the texts of the Berlin composer's cycle. In the list of Berger's Müller settings below, the initial number is that of the song's order in the set of ten.

1. Des Müllers Wanderlied. ('Ich hört' ein Bächlein rauschen', later entitled 'Wohin?');
2. Müllers Blumen. (later entitled 'Des Müllers Blumen');
7. Der Müller. ('Ich möchte ziehn in die Welt hinaus', later entitled 'Die böse Farbe');

9. Müllers trockne Blumen. (later entitled 'Trock'ne Blumen');
10. Des Baches Lied. (later entitled 'Des Baches Wiegenlied')

Berger's cycle thus begins, not with 'Das Wandern' but with the earliest published version of 'Wohin?', lacking the later third verse.

Early versions of the six other poems from *Die schöne Müllerin* were also published in *Der Gesellschafter* within the week from 30 May to 6 June. 'Der Neugierige' and 'Mein!' appeared in the edition for 30 May 1818, the latter very unlike its later incarnation:

Das schönste Lied (The most beautiful song)

Bächlein, laß dein Rauschen,	Little brook, stop your babbling!
Räder, steht nur still!	Mill-wheels, stand still!
Kommt heran zu lauschen,	Come here and listen, whoever wishes to
Wer das schönste Liedchen hören will!	hear the most beautiful little song of all!
Still, ihr Nachtigallen	Be quiet, nightingales!
Lerchen, Finken, still!	Larks and finches, cease your singing!
Laß ein eitel Schallen	Leave off your vain efforts to make music,
Wer das schönste Liedchen hören will!	whoever would hear the most beautiful little song of all!
Sonne, gib herunter	Sun, give forth
Deinen hellsten Schein;	your most brilliant rays;
Frühling, strahle bunter:	Springtime, shine merrily:
Die geliebte Müllerin ist mein!	The beloved miller maid is mine!

The latter version unfurls to greater lengths, its ecstasy less terse, and the awkward refrain of the earlier version is eliminated. Most important of all the revisions to this poem, the ending is altered and considerably deepened.

The completed cycle

Müller's pre-Italian cycle of 1817 consisted of the following poems, listed here in the chronological order of the narrative – he did not publish the work as a full-fledged narrative cycle until the *Waldhornisten-Gedichte*.

1. Wanderschaft
2. Wohin?
3. Der Neugierige
4. Des Müllers Blumen
5. Am Feierabend
6. Mein
7. Ein ungereimtes Lied
8. Der Jäger

9. Eifersucht und Stolz
10. Erster Schmerz, letzter Scherz
11. Die liebe Farbe
12. Die böse Farbe
13. Trock'ne Blumen
14. Der Müller und der Bach
15. Des Baches Wiegenlied

At some unknown time after his return to Dessau, perhaps in spring or early summer 1820, Müller added the following ten poems: 'Der Dichter als Prolog', 'Halt!', 'Danksagung an den Bach', 'Das Mühlenleben', 'Ungeduld', 'Morgengruß', 'Pause', 'Mit dem grünen Lautenbande', 'Blümlein Vergißmein', and 'Der Dichter als Epilog'. With the cycle completed, Müller read the finished work in July 1820 to a small group of friends that included the great Romantic writer Ludwig Tieck, Müller's friend and supporter.[21] Tieck did not like the tragic ending, but he found the rest praiseworthy and encouraged Müller to publish the work. The *Waldhornisten-Gedichte I* subsequently sold well and, with some exceptions, was favourably reviewed, although one critic rightly points out the uneven quality of the poems – 'Reduce the book by half', he said, 'and its acclaim would be greater', a judgement in which modern readers have concurred. Despite such caveats from certain critics, the book sold well. Müller published a second edition in 1826 and dedicated it to Tieck, in gratitude for his support.

Müller conceived much of his verse as poetry for music, and he was especially pleased when composers set his poems to music. Shortly after his twenty-first birthday in 1815, he wrote an imaginary address to E. T. A. Hoffmann's fictional Kapellmeister Kreisler in his diary:

I can neither play nor sing, yet when I write verses, I sing and play after all. If I could produce the melodies, my songs would be more pleasing than they are now. But courage! perhaps there is a kindred spirit somewhere who will hear the tunes behind the words and give them back to me.[22]

When the composer Bernhard Josef Klein (1793–1832) published his settings of six poems by Müller in 1822, including a setting of 'Trock'ne Blumen' extracted from the complete cycle, the poet wrote in a letter of thanks, 'For indeed my songs lead but half a life, a paper existence of black-and-white, until music breathes life into them, or at least calls it forth and awakens it if it is already dormant in them.'[23] Other composers found his verse eminently suited for music, including Fanny Mendelssohn-Hensel, Carl Maria von Weber, Carl Loewe, Louis Spohr, Giacomo Meyerbeer, and Johannes Brahms, as well as many lesser lights. Müller's greatest 'kindred spirit', however, was Schubert, a composer he never knew, who indeed 'heard the tunes within the words', and gave them back to the world.

2

Schubert and the genesis of the music

Schubert's illness

1823, the year in which Schubert composed *Die schöne Müllerin*, D. 795, was a turning point in his life, a time fraught with crisis. The venereal disease, probably syphilis, that was to kill him five years later first became evident in late 1822 or early 1823, and its initial virulent stages wracked the composer's health for much of that year.[1] For all the chronological mysteries and gaps in the chronicle, we know that the genesis of the cycle is interwoven with the beginning of the end of Schubert's life.

Despite the compound of the respect accorded genius and a linguistic veil of nineteenth-century euphemisms, three of Schubert's contemporaries, speaking in guarded terms, identify the cause of his illness as venereal disease and attribute his early death to its ravages. Joseph Kenner, writing in 1858, is possibly biased by his hatred of Franz von Schober, whom he blames for leading Schubert astray. 'Anyone who knew Schubert', he writes, 'knows how he was made of two natures, foreign to each other, how powerfully the craving for pleasure dragged his soul down to the slough of moral degradation, and how highly he valued the utterances of friends he respected . . . [this] episode in Schubert's life . . . only too probably caused his premature death and certainly hastened it' (*Memoirs*, 86). The unsympathetic Wilhelm von Chézy in 1863 wrote that Schubert 'had strayed into those wrong paths which generally admit of no return, at least of no healthy one' and adds that 'The charming "Müllerlieder" were composed under sufferings of a quite different kind from those immortalized in the music which he put into the mouth of the poor lovelorn miller lad' (*Memoirs*, 261). Schober himself spoke in discreet terms of Schubert's hospitalization 'as the result of excessively indulgent sensual living and its consequences' (*Memoirs*, 266). These and other references to a streak of 'coarse sensuality' in Schubert's character have led the modern scholar Maynard Solomon to speculate convincingly that Schubert was a sexually promiscuous homosexual who chose to spend his brief adulthood within the protective environs of the gay subculture of Biedermeier Vienna.[2]

Whatever the full truth of the matter, the piper came due in 1823. Schubert would have known that the disease spelled the ruin of his health for whatever length of time remained to him and that it would lead to his death. We have only scattered references to his ill health and to the mill songs by which to trace a tentative chronology of the inception of *Die schöne Müllerin* and the early course of the disease. Schubert himself first mentions illness in a formal letter of 28 February 1823 to one Councillor Mosel, to whom Schubert had sent part of his opera *Alfonso und Estrella*: 'the circumstances of my health still do not permit me to leave the house'.[3] His words suggest that he was under medical quarantine because of the highly infective nature of primary syphilis, which Eric Sams speculates was first manifest some time between mid-January and mid-February. Were that so, the next round of symptoms in the customary timetable for the disease would occur in late April and May, possibly triggering a renewed outbreak of despair. In his diary (now lost) for 8 May 1823, Schubert wrote a poem entitled 'Mein Gebet' (My Prayer), one of his few extant essays in poetry, with desperation in every line. The anti-clerical composer is shocked into pleading with God for death and rebirth after the 'unheard-of grief' that is now his lot (*Documents*, 279). *Die schöne Müllerin* was composed against the backdrop of this new and terrible realization; in fact, he composed the first songs, in all likelihood, soon after the composition of this heart-wrenching prayer. On 31 March 1824, the year in which the cycle was published, he wrote to Leopold Kupelwieser:

Imagine a man whose health will never be right again, and who in sheer despair over this ever makes things worse and worse, instead of better; imagine a man, I say, whose most brilliant hopes have perished, to whom the felicity of love and friendship have nothing to offer but pain at best, whom enthusiasm ... for all things beautiful threatens to forsake, and I ask you, is he not a miserable, unhappy being? (*Documents*, 339)

One not only imagines the pain with which he wrote such words, but hears it thereafter resound in his music, beneath even the sunniest and most serene surfaces.

The compositional history of the song cycle

The detailed chronology of *Die schöne Müllerin* is unclear, especially its inception. The autograph engraver's copy of the complete cycle is almost entirely missing. Only no. 15, 'Eifersucht u[nd]. Stolz', dated and signed

'October 1823 Frz. Schubert mpia [manu propria]', has survived – Schubert apparently gave it to a Countess Marie Wimpffen, born Freiin von Eskeles – and is now in the Vienna Gesellschaft der Musikfreunde (manuscript A 232).[4] In a letter to Franz Schober of 30 November 1823, Schubert wrote, 'I have composed nothing since the opera except a few mill-songs. The mill-songs will appear in four books, with vignettes by Schwind.' The cycle was eventually published in five booklets, not four, and, unfortunately, without the promised engravings by his friend Moritz von Schwind (1804–71), the artist to whom we owe some of the most treasured images of Schubert and his circle. (The opera Schubert refers to is *Fierabras*, D. 796, begun on 25 May and completed on 2 October.) Both the dated first draft and the letter, with its reference to 'a *few* mill-songs' (italics mine), would seem to confirm that Schubert composed the last few songs – how many, one wonders, is 'a few'? – in October and November, thus completing a cycle begun earlier. But when? According to Josef von Spaun and Franz Schober, Schubert composed some of the songs while in the hospital, but they do not say when he was hospitalized (*Memoirs*, 367 and 266). Walther Dürr has hypothesized that this was in October, after Schubert's return to Vienna, but Franz von Hartmann writes of hearing Schubert and the great singer Johann Michael Vogl (1768–1840), a leading light of the Vienna court opera from 1795 to 1821, perform some of the mill-songs in Linz on 28 July (*Memoirs*, 273).[5] John Reed points out the conspicuous gap in the record during June and July (no dated autographs, no outings or visits) and suggests that the crisis of the disease and the inception of the miller cycle perhaps both occurred at that time.[6] On 26 July the artist Leopold Kupelwieser wrote to Schober with the news that Schubert was ill, and another friend of Schober's wrote on 12 November about his visit to Steyr in late August/early September to visit 'our dear little Tubby': 'I found him seriously ill at the time, but you know that anyhow' (*Documents*, 284 and 296). Schubert himself wrote to Schober on 14 August 1823, 'I correspond busily with [August von] Schäffer [the first of the Viennese physicians who treated Schubert] and remain fairly well. I almost despair of ever becoming entirely well again' (*Documents*, 286). During his holiday, he worked on *Fierabras* and possibly only resumed work on the cycle upon his return.

Die schöne Müllerin, Op. 25 was published in 1824 in five booklets by the firm of Sauer & Leidesdorf and dedicated to Karl Freiherr von Schönstein (born the same year as Schubert, 1797–1876), an accomplished amateur singer with 'a beautiful, noble-sounding, high baritone voice' whom Schubert had met at Zseliz in 1818 and who became a friend and ardent supporter of Schubert's songs (from Leopold von Sonnleithner's 1857 reminiscences in *Memoirs*, 117). According to Schönstein's reminiscences in 1857, he had sung only Italian music before meeting Schubert, after which he devoted himself almost exclusively to German song and especially to Schubert's works (*Memoirs*, 100–1). Franz Liszt heard Schönstein sing in Vienna in 1838 and declared himself moved to tears: 'Baron Schönstein declaims Schubert's songs with the technique of a great artist and sings them with the simple sensitivity of an amateur who concentrates on the emotions expressed [in the songs], without preoccupying himself with the public.'[7] From this and other testimonials, it seems that Schönstein sang in an unembellished, natural manner, without dramatic effects. In Schwind's famous sepia drawing of *A Schubert Evening at Josef von Spaun's*, Schönstein is depicted as a handsome, moustachioed young man standing just behind Johann Michael Vogl and Schubert, both at the piano. The drawing dates from 1868 and is therefore a monument to memory, doubtless idealized, but looking at it, one imagines Vogl and Schönstein taking turns to sing Schubert's songs while the composer himself accompanies them. Especially to the last remaining members of the Schubert circle and the Vienna that had known composer and singer alike in their heyday, Schönstein and *Die schöne Müllerin* were linked together: in 1866, Schwind still wrote letters to him as 'Baron Schönstein, Journeyman Miller'.

The first booklet of the cycle, containing songs 1–4, was announced in the principal Viennese newspaper of the day, the *Wiener Zeitung*, for 17 February 1824, and the second booklet, containing songs 5–9, was announced as available for purchase on 24 March. The remainder of the cycle did not appear until mid-August (the announcement of the third, fourth, and fifth booklets, containing songs nos. 10–12, 13–17, and 18–20 respectively, was printed on 12 August), and Schubert, who spent the summer in Zseliz at the home of the Esterházy family, had grown impatient with the delay. Schubert's father wrote to his son at the end of June 1824, saying, 'Your brother Ferdinand spoke to Herr [Maximilian Joseph] Leidesdorf and got from him for correction the songs of yours he is about to publish, which Leidesdorf was on the point of sending you for that purpose' (*Documents*, 356). From this letter, we learn that Ferdinand proofread the last three books, or songs 10–20, in Schubert's stead, which explains the unusual number of errors in the first edition. 'Eifersucht und Stolz' is especially fault-ridden – perhaps understandably, as this is an extremely complex song. Schubert wrote to Ferdinand sometime between 16 and 18 July, reproaching his brother for not writing and expressing concern about the lack of news from Leidesdorf, whom he characterizes as 'rather negligent by nature' (*Documents*, 362).[8] Schubert was evidently scanning the *Wiener Zeitung* for the announcement of book 3 and was displeased when he did not find it.

When the final three booklets were at last published, the cycle met with less success than he had anticipated. Schober wrote him a sympathetic letter on 2 December 1824, saying 'And your miller songs have also brought no great acclaim? These hounds [the public] have no feelings or minds of their own and they blindly follow the noise and the opinions of others' (*Documents*, 386). Schubert's reputation as a master song composer had already been established before the publication of the first Müller cycle in 1824, so he had every reason to expect an interested public to flock around so rich an offering. In the announcement of his Opp. 12–14 songs in the *Wiener Zeitung* for 13 December 1822, he was characterized as 'the ingenious composer who in so short a time has become a favourite with connoisseurs and amateurs', and Beethoven's conversation book for August 1823 includes the tantalizing sentence 'They greatly praise Schubert, but it is said that he hides himself', written by Beethoven's nephew Karl (*Documents*, 251 and 288). Whether 'they' denotes a specific group of people or a general, amorphous designation, it is clear that Schubert at the age of twenty-seven was a popular and well-respected composer. However, there seem to have been no reviews of Op. 25 in the Viennese, Berlin, Leipzig, etc. music journals and newspapers during Schubert's lifetime, such as one finds for *Winterreise* in 1828, and Schubert was both puzzled and aggrieved by the curious absence of notice. In the introduction to ch. 3, I have speculated that an element of the poetic narrative – the miller's effeminacy – could possibly have been a factor in the work's slow start. The cycle of course *did* become enormously popular after Schubert's death; once the cycle 'caught on' with the public, numerous copies in domestic songbooks of the period and arrangements attest to its popularity.[9] His long-standing friend Josef von Spaun, in his 1864 reminiscences, writes that 'The five books of the Müllerlieder alone, for which Schubert received a mere bagatelle [Spaun exaggerates], brought the publisher such a large profit, through repeated editions, that he was able to buy a house with it' (*Memoirs*, 356). Beyond monetary reward, Schubert might reasonably have expected someone somewhere to notice that he had extended the concert song cycle, the younger cousin of the *Liederspiel*, to new lengths and new profundity.

Sources, copies, and the second edition

Regrettably, almost all of the autograph sources for the cycle have vanished, and so too have most of the copies made by members of Schubert's circle. Schubert made a fair copy of nos. 7–9 for Karl von Schönstein, all three songs transposed downwards, probably to conform more comfortably to his friend's high baritone voice ('Ungeduld' in F major and with the tempo marking 'Lebhaft', 'Morgengruß' in A major, and 'Des Müllers Blumen' in G major).[10] At the end of no. 9, Schubert reportedly wrote 'The accompaniment to this song may conveniently be played an octave higher'; clearly, he was not particularly fastidious about such matters in performance. One cannot imagine Schumann or Hugo Wolf – especially Wolf! – sanctioning anything of the kind. The manuscript has since disappeared, along with the autograph engraver's copy of all but 'Eifersucht und Stolz' and a complete copy of the cycle made by Karl von Schönstein and signed 'Schönstein 869', in the private collection of Hans Laufer in London until 1959.

The first edition is thus the foremost source close to the composer for most of the twenty songs. In his critical notes to the edition of the cycle in the *Neue Schubert-Ausgabe*, Walther Dürr lists the errors in the first edition, errors especially numerous in songs 10–20 proofread by Ferdinand rather than Franz, and there is no need for me to recount more than a single revealing example of brotherly carelessness or lack of comprehension. The original fault was, of course, the engraver's, but Ferdinand, a composer of lesser gifts than his brother, failed to spot misprints such as those in the following passage from 'Eifersucht und Stolz' (Ex. 1). In the engraver's copy, Schubert had indicated the repetition of the right-hand figure in bars 26–7 by means of the common abbreviation sign for repeated figures, and yet the printer, as if not believing what he saw, substitutes a more conventional triadic pattern. Ferdinand, who perhaps did not have access to the autograph manuscript at the time, subsequently saw nothing wrong with the passage. Whatever his brother's deficiencies as a proofreader, however, Schubert relied on him, not only for such practical matters as this but also for emotional support in the dark days of 1823–4. 'I feel more clearly than ever at this moment', he wrote in July 1824, 'that you, and you only, are my truest friend, bound to my soul with every fibre!' (*Memoirs*, 363). Four years later, he died in Ferdinand's apartment and in his brother's care.

In 1830, little more than a year after the composer's death, Anton Diabelli brought out a second edition of *Die schöne Müllerin*, an edition that has provoked considerable controversy in both the nineteenth and the

Ex. 1

twentieth centuries.[11] Max Friedländer, the editor of the first complete Schubert edition, and others in the late nineteenth century condemned the Diabelli edition as corrupt and filled with 'falsifications', but it is actually a fascinating record of the performance practices of contemporary Austrian singers in general and Vogl in particular: the *Veränderungen* and *Manieren* (alterations and ornamental embellishments) in the Diabelli edition are of his devising.[12] Schober, who knew how greatly Schubert admired the singer's artistry as Orestes in Gluck's *Iphigénie en Tauride*, arranged for the two men to meet in early 1817; Vogl, recognizing the younger man's genius, quickly became his friend, fellow-artist, adviser, and an enthusiastic proponent of his songs. For the remainder of Schubert's life and of his own, Vogl strove wholeheartedly, if perhaps with an understandable element of self-interest – Schubert's songs clearly gave his singing career a new lease of life – to convert the concert-going public to lieder, especially Schubert's lieder, in place of the arias expected of well-known singers on recital programmes, to take the lied from the domain of *Hausmusik* to the recital hall. In the letter in which Schubert tells Schober about the completion of the miller songs, he also writes that 'Vogl is taken up with my songs almost exclusively. He writes out the voice-part himself and, so to speak, lives on it' (*Documents*, 301). He did not, however, copy Schubert's melodies exactly as he received them from the composer. From the evidence of a collection of 'Lieder von Franz Schubert und Reichardt, verändert von M. Vogl' (Songs by Schubert and Reichardt, altered by Vogl) in the Gesellschaft der Musikfreunde and the Diabelli edition of *Die schöne Müllerin*, the famous singer carefully wrote down his embellishments to Schubert's music.[13]

It is possible, Robert Schollum speculates, that Vogl was the first singer to apply to the German lieder art the kind of interpretative freedom that was an expected element of opera.[14] Vogl did indeed avail himself of multiple musical liberties: his *Manieren*, that is, a performer's added ornaments and variants, include scalar motion to fill in larger intervals, turning figures and trills, high notes raised still higher or lowered for greater ease of singing, dotted rhythms and inserted rests to make the declamation more dramatic, changes to the dynamic markings, ties, and slurs, even alterations to the melody and harmonies. Whether these alterations and embellishments stemmed from the operatic 'Italianità' regnant in Vienna or were in general use among singers has been a matter of scholarly controversy, but such procedures were a generally accepted aspect of vocal performance practice. Free handling of the musical material by performers was so commonplace that its application to the lied did not excite much comment at the time. Only later, when Schubert had become sacrosanct, the patron saint of lieder, and the pendulum of musical fashion had swung away from improvised ornamentation, did controversy over the embellished edition arise.

Schubert of course knew of the emendations in Vogl's performances of his songs, but how he felt about the matter is less sure. Although Vogl's influence on Schubert is beyond doubt (the gifted actor reportedly made a practice on occasion of declaiming the composer's chosen poems before Schubert set them to music) and most of the Schubert circle praised Vogl lavishly for the sensitivity and profundity of his performances, at least one witness testified to occasional controversy between the composer and singer over Vogl's *Manieren*. The Viennese playwright Eduard Bauernfeld, a member of the Schubert circle in the composer's later years (he did not know Schubert personally in 1823) and not always the most reliable witness, wrote in his 'Memoir of J. M. Vogl' (1841): 'Small alterations and embellishments, which the skilful singer, a past master of effect, allowed himself, received the composer's consent to some extent, but not infrequently they also gave rise to friendly controversy' (*Documents*, 226). Leopold von Sonnleithner also wrote that Vogl 'overstepped the permissible limits [separating the lyric manner Sonnleithner believed proper to lieder from dramatic style] more and more as he lost his voice, but nevertheless he always sang *strictly in time*; and he merely helped himself out as well as he could, in the manner of the experienced opera singer, where his voice and strength did not suffice' (*Memoirs*, 116–17). Schubert's friends testify over and over again to their admiration for Vogl's interpretative skills, and Schubert himself wrote from Gmunden to his brother Ferdinand about a salon performance he and Vogl had given there in 1825: 'The manner in which Vogl sings and I accompany, as though we were one at such a moment, is something quite new and unheard-of for these people' (letter of 12 September 1825, *Documents*, 458). It is conceivable that Schubert would have willingly sacrificed some of his compositional individuality in order to become 'one' musically with a great performer who laboured so devotedly on his behalf. There were no manuals for vocal embellishment; musical understanding, taste, and vocal technique alone dictated the performer's embellishments of a work, and Vogl, a man of great culture, was no vulgar virtuoso. If some of the reports of his singing are true, however, he was given to dramatic interpretations, and he was fifty-five years old when Schubert composed *Die schöne Müllerin*. Without disparaging his efforts on Schubert's behalf, it is possible that some of his alterations to Schubert's music were made in compensation for the lessened breath and lowered range of an ageing operatic voice.

Vogl left few songs untouched, although there *are* exceptions and his emendations were relatively modest.[15] 'Halt!' and 'Morgengruß' are, somewhat surprisingly, unembellished (he could, of course, have ornamented them in performance), and 'Der Jäger', not surprisingly, is also left as is, surely because the music leaves no time or space for it. I shall mention only a few representative examples of the alterations in the second edition to demonstrate in some small measure how Schubert may have heard his own work interpreted in all the freshness of its first years on earth, beginning with bars 19–20 of 'Das Wandern'. Where Schubert's miller softly echoes the words 'das Wandern, das Wandern', Vogl consigns the echo to the piano and adds a turning figure to the vocal cadence. In 'Wohin?', Vogl sang the successive phrases 'Was sag' ich denn vom Rauschen?' and 'Das kann kein Rauschen sein' beginning on the downbeat, thus accenting the words 'Was' and 'Das' rather than the verbs 'sag' and 'kann'. In this way, Vogl rhythmically underscores the syntactical change from declarative statements to a question, but Schubert's downbeat stress on the verb 'to say' seems far more apt for a poet-singer like the miller. The same alteration can also be found in 'Mit dem grünen Lautenbande' at the words '*Nun* hab' das Grüne gern', probably in order to put interpretative stress on the word 'now'. Ends of songs are particularly prone to embellishment, as in the ornamented final vocal cadence of 'Danksagung an den Bach' and the gratuitous high A♯ added to the final vocal phrase of 'Der Neugierige'. He may have made certain alterations for greater ease of singing: for example, he eliminates the jubilant figures at the words 'Durch den Hain / Aus und ein' in 'Mein!' – one of the most heavily emended songs in the Diabelli edition – and substitutes a simpler, less athletic phrase (Ex. 2).

Looking at 'Eifersucht und Stolz', one can imagine Schubert remonstrating with Vogl for taking excessive liberties with the score, as in Bauernfeld's anecdote. Embellishments and various melodic-rhythmic alterations for heightened declamatory effect are one thing, but distorting the form through the addition of extra bars is another. After the words 'lustig zieht nach Haus' and 'den Kopf zum Fenster 'naus', Diabelli–Vogl repeats the fanfare in the piano but transposed an octave higher, thereby adding an extra two bars to the song. Presumably for added dramatic effect, the singer is directed to prolong the word 'doch' in the phrase 'Doch sag ihr nicht' for an entire bar, preceded by an extra bar in the piano; where Schubert repeats a G major chord for two bars (bars 55–6), Diabelli–Vogl has four bars. Schubert's brief, gasping breath, so wonderfully expressive of urgency, at the comma separating the words 'Hörst du, kein Wort', becomes a pause of more than a bar, while the piano spins out an extra bar of the dominant harmony (Ex. 3). To a late-modern purist mentality, this is really going too far. As nineteenth-century tastes shifted and greater adherence to the composer's notated wishes became fashionable, one can trace a gradual purging of the score through subsequent editions, beginning

Ex. 2

with the 'corrected' edition on which Benedikt Randhartinger worked *circa* 1860, published by Diabelli's successor Carl Anton Spina in 1864 (this was what ignited the controversy), and leading eventually to Max Friedländer's edition for Peters in 1884.[16] In an earlier Peters edition, undated but post-1869, the editor tells the buying public that the second Viennese edition was filled with numerous emendations that did not originate with the composer, 'as the newest research has shown'. Vogl is not mentioned.

The premiere of the cycle

It seems incredible when one recounts it, but *Die schöne Müllerin* was not performed in its entirety in a public recital until 1856, thirty-two years after its first appearance in print. The programming practices of nineteenth-century musicians were largely responsible for the delay, since variety – a veritable hodge-podge at times – reigns over unity in contemporary concert programmes. One of the reviewers of *Winterreise*, dubious about the very existence of the genre, wrote that he preferred 'individual blossoms' of song to entire garlands, and he was not alone in his opinion.[17] Composers typically chose only a poem or two from the miller cycle; Otto Claudius's *Neun Lieder von Wilhelm Müller* (Leipzig: Breitkopf & Härtel, 1833) is an exception to the usual practice, and Schubert's is the only near-complete setting.[18] Well into the present century, singers have plucked favourite blossoms, such as 'Ungeduld' from *Die schöne Müllerin* or 'Der Lindenbaum'

Ex. 3

Kopf zum Fen-ster n'aus.   Wenn von dem

Fang der Jä - ger lu - stig zieht nach Haus.

Es steckt kein sitt - sam Kind den Kopf zum Fen - ster

(Ex. 3 continued)

n'aus, geh Bäch - lein hin und sag' ihr das, geh Bächlein

hin und sag' ihr das.

Doch   sag ihr nicht

from *Winterreise*, and performed them as individual lieder, apart from the larger structure to which they belong.

In May of 1856, the famous singer Julius Stockhausen (1826–1906, born in Switzerland only two years before Schubert's death and a student in Paris of the great Spanish tenor Manuel Garcia) gave three concerts in Vienna under Spina's auspices; Spina, as Diabelli's successor, had an understandable interest in promoting sales of his edition of the score. Stockhausen, whom Brahms once called 'the most musical of all the singers', began the series with a concert announced in the *Wiener Zeitung* for Thursday 1 May, a conventional programme of lieder, ballads (then *de rigueur*), Italian and French arias in which he nevertheless paved the way for the radical novelty of an entire song cycle performed integrally by including 'Wohin?', 'Der Neugierige', and 'Der Müller und der Bach'. For his second and third concerts on Tuesday the 6th and Thursday the 8th, he sang only *Die schöne Müllerin* (what edition, one wonders, did he use?). Eduard Hanslick, the powerful critic of the *Neue Freie Presse*, was struck by the novelty:

> Stockhausen bade farewell to the public with what is truly the simplest programme in the world. Instead of the usual omnium gatherum of pieces that do not belong together and have nothing to do with one another, we read on the announcement only: 'Die schöne Müllerin, a song cycle by Franz Schubert'. The idea is, to our knowledge, a new one.[19]

For Hanslick (and, one must imagine, others in the recital hall, filled to capacity), it was a welcome revelation to hear the cycle brought to life as a totality, to hear the relationships only perceptible when the sequence is performed in order.[20] It is a revealing review: Hanslick is never dull to read, and he may well be the chief instigator of Müller's fall from grace among musicians, although his dissatisfaction with the poet follows later. In 1856, for the benefit of those unacquainted with the complete text because of the traditional piecemeal performance – a song here, a song there – he summarizes the 'simple little novel in song', missing its subtleties altogether and seeing in it only naive, folk-like fodder for musical setting. However, Hanslick perceptively points out that Schubert did not always pay such scrupulous attention to the poetry as his ardent adherents would have one believe. Rather, his musical inspiration often ran roughshod over the poet's images. As an example, Hanslick writes that Schubert sets the opening words of 'Die böse Farbe' ('Ich möchte ziehen in die Welt hinaus') briskly and energetically, as if the singer were a bold adventurer or a knight bent on great deeds rather than a lad weighted down by grief and oppressed by love's sorrow. Ludwig Berger's *Agitato* setting of 'Der Müller' in E minor was, in Hanslick's opinion, closer to Müller's meaning and atmosphere than Schubert's, but his musical talents were so much more limited than those of his Vienna contemporary that the two songs are hardly of comparable worth.

By 1860, however, when Stockhausen again performed the whole of *Die schöne Müllerin* in Vienna, the novelty had palled, and Hanslick turned against performance of entire cycles, by extension, against recitals of nothing but lieder (*Liederabende*), with a vengeance. Although he reassures the Viennese Schubert-worshippers that the mill songs are among the best in all of German music, nevertheless, such a 'monster concert' waxes monotonous. Hanslick particularly objected to the 'false sentimentality' of Müller's poetry. By the end, the mill-wheels, he says, are driven by a flood of tears, and even the most *gemütlich* listener becomes hard of heart. Evidently, an actress named Frau Rettich gave a dramatic reading of Müller's Prologue and Epilogue (the three omitted poems are not mentioned) at the beginning and end of the evening, and Hanslick has a withering last word for these 'unbearably precious' poems: 'One could hardly put the beloved images of our mill to worse shame than by planting these scarecrows before and after.'[21] Thus begins the decline in Müller's reputation among musicians. Did the famous critic's scorn also contribute to snuffing out the *Liederabend* in Vienna for a generation thereafter? Not until the 1880s did a new fad for song evenings – nothing but lieder – reappear in Vienna.

Hanslick's reservations, and his witty vitriol in prose, did not keep Stockhausen from performing the cycle in its entirety elsewhere, to large audiences and great acclaim. Brahms, who dedicated his *Romanzen aus Ludwig Tiecks Magelone*, Op. 33, to Stockhausen, was Stockhausen's accompanist on 19 and 24 April 1861 in performances of *Die schöne Müllerin* in Hamburg and Altona, and the composer, conductor, and pedagogue Ferdinand Hiller was his accompanist for a performance in Cologne in 1862 to an audience of 2,000 people. For a concert in St Petersburg in 1866 featuring Henryk Wieniawski, Anton Rubinstein, and Stockhausen, Stockhausen sang both Schumann's Eichendorff *Liederkreis*, Op. 39 and *Die schöne Müllerin* in a programme that also included a Beethoven piano trio and an unspecified piano solo.[22] Not for the first time, one wishes that recording equipment had been invented earlier than it was.

1 Alfred Roller, 'Guten Morgen, schöne Müllerin', India ink illustration for a Schubert ball, Vienna 1897, reproduced with permission of the Historisches Museum der Stadt Wien.

In conclusion: little-known illustrations of the cycle

On the occasion of a municipal ball held in Vienna in 1897 to celebrate the centenary of Schubert's birth, souvenir booklets with illustrations by some of the leading Viennese artists of the day were given to the ladies attending the ball. Those pen-and-ink drawings included a depiction of 'Morgengruß' by Alfred Roller (1864–1935), a founding member of the Vienna Secession and revolutionary stage designer at the State Opera House under Gustav Mahler and with Max Reinhardt in Berlin (Roller's drawing strongly resembles a sketch for a stage set), and an illustration of 'Tränenregen' by Rudolf Bacher (1862–1943), a painter, sculptor, and professor at the Academy of Fine Arts.[23] In both illustrations, one notices the androgynous depiction of the miller, his tender, yearning aspect scarcely less girlish than the miller maid herself. Tellingly, their eyes never meet: Bacher's lily-maiden, gowned in white and carrying a flower-trimmed hat, looks at the miller, but he looks down into the water, while Roller's miller gazes fervently at a maiden who is not turned towards him and does not look in his direction. Neither the youth nor the maiden is depicted as an individual in either drawing; they are generically pretty *fin-de-siècle* versions of Youth Masculine (sort of) and Feminine. Both artists, I believe, found visual equivalents for important elements of the poetic narrative,

28

2 Rudolf Bacher, 'Wir saßen so traulich beisammen', India ink drawing, reproduced with permission of the Historisches Museum der Stadt Wien.

even though the illustrations are at least as expressive of their own era as they are of Müller's and Schubert's cycles. In Carl Schorske's memorable phrase, Schubert's Vienna seemed a Biedermeier Paradise Lost to the anxious inhabitants of a latter-day culture on the way to disintegration.[24] Are Roller's and Bacher's interpretations consonant with Müller's poetic themes and their development in *Die schöne Müllerin*, despite the distortion through a *fin-de-siècle* glass? We shall see in the next chapter.

3

Romantic illusions: the poetic texts, nos. 1–12

Introduction

Neither the characters nor the plot of what became *Die schöne Müllerin* are original, as we have seen. What saves the cycle from being merely a compilation of warmed-up scraps are Müller's poetic skill and his often subtle scepticism towards his Romantic inheritance. The parenthetical subtitle '(Im Winter zu lesen)', or 'To read in the winter', that Müller added when he published the complete cycle in the *Waldhornisten-Gedichte I* reflects that scepticism from the start. He was fond of balanced polarities, and therefore the cycle that follows *Die schöne Müllerin* bears the corresponding subtitle '(To read in the springtime)', but the wintry designation for his miller poems is significant. Müller was a latecomer, someone who followed on the heels of Romanticism's golden age and could no longer speak as a true Romantic. He knew many of its poets and borrowed their images, but he and his characters are outsiders who find much in Romanticism an oddity to be questioned and misunderstood, even where they most yearn for its former verities and echo, in wistful or mocking disbelief, its themes. From the winter of post-Romantic disillusionment, he looked back at the springtime of Romantic ideals across a chasm he could not traverse.[1]

Die schöne Müllerin is a narrative, but one told in a distinctive way. Müller seemingly suppresses the narrating voice in his mill story, that is, someone other than the principal characters who is responsible for a share of the story-telling, in order to write monodrama with a single speaker: the miller, *not* 'the beautiful miller maid' of the title. She is an icon in the mind – a *Frauenbild*, as the wanderer in *Die Winterreise* tellingly dubs his former sweetheart in 'Die Wetterfahne'. The less we see and hear of the miller maid, the more the miller can worship her, unimpeded by actuality. The tale ostensibly reaches us through the warping filter of his perceptions alone, shaped and limited by needs, biases, and desires that we must extract from his words in order to know him better than he knows himself.

Accordingly, the plot is sketchy, merely the poetic adumbration of a narrative. One can divide the story into the following episodes – the miller goes wandering, the awakening of love, his hopes for love's realization, the delusion that his love is reciprocated, the arrival of the hunter and the miller maid's attraction to him, the miller's despair and death – but of these stages along the way, we hear only what evokes the miller's emotions at that moment. Of the other characters (miller maid, father, hunter, the other mill-workers), the place, the passage of time, and what happens between the poems, we hear only what he chooses to recount, from which we extrapolate that which he *fails* to notice, hear, or see. This version of a familiar literary scenario no longer seems so simple when one realizes that Müller experiments with blurring the gap between events reported along a chronological continuum – that is, a plot made up of certainties – and lyric poetry's emphasis on emotion, belief, experience.

There *are* other voices in the cycle, however, including one that Schubert omits. As in all monodrama, one catches strategic glimpses of the author himself, whose world-view is different from that of the speaker, behind the words but not as a presence in the foreground. Like the puppet-master behind the scenes, he juxtaposes reality and delusion within the tale so that the reader can distinguish between them, even if the miller cannot; the judgement on the miller maid's personality that one finds at the end of 'Tränenregen' issues from the author, not the besotted young man. Far more obvious is the fictive Poet (not the same as a narrator, but rather someone who *interprets* the other voices for the reader) who speaks in the Prologue and Epilogue that frame the cycle on either side. The Poet instructs his readers, to whom he speaks as if they were playgoers attending the theatre, that none of this is real; poets, he tells them, play with words as with stage props. It is no wonder that Schubert, acting in the venerable tradition of the composer as poet's editor, omitted both the subtitle and the Prologue and Epilogue in which the sense of ironic distance between the poet and his subject is most acute. 'The Poet' vanishes, to be replaced by 'The Composer', who has different plans for *his* audience.

The Poet's sarcasm is a defensive stratagem, since he and the miller are actually close kin. Both are poets, although the miller does not identify himself as one until midway through the cycle, and Romantic poets are suspect in gender, effeminized masculine presences. Müller's reminiscence of the lovelorn Ophelia – rosemary for remembrance and symbolic greenery for the grave – for his lovelorn *male* character in 'Die liebe Farbe' underscores the ambiguities of gender in this cycle. It is usually

32

women who are represented in literature as pining for the love of men who
ignore them, women who go mad for lack of love, who abase themselves
and plead for the lover's return, who lament their pain aloud rather than
masking it in traditional male stoicism, who kill themselves when all hope
of his love is lost. In the non-contest with a rival identified almost solely by
his animal virility, the miller sets the seal on his own effeminacy. His
diminished masculinity may, all in the realm of speculation, have influ-
enced Tieck's disapproval of the tragic ending, the slow initial response to
Schubert's setting of the cycle, and the misogynistic Hanslick's dislike of
poetry he deemed too sickly-sweet to bear.[2] Sentiment, that is, the display-
ing of feeling, is not traditionally the province of 'manly men', scornful of
lyric poetry. The Poet, with his know-it-all Stage Manager's demeanour
and iambic pentameters laden with orotund male authority, displaces onto
the miller the burden of sentiment and briskly disavows its connection with
his own world – until the Epilogue.

In sum, *Die schöne Müllerin* is the poetic narration of romantic/Romantic
passion, a myth Müller simultaneously celebrates and questions. Like
Tristan, the miller does not love the miller maid for herself, but because he
desires Love itself, of which her beauty is the image. Passion of this kind is
at bottom narcissism, the lover's self-magnification, rather than a relation
with the beloved, and it is closely intertwined with the longing for death.
The miller of course does not recognize the nature of his soul-sickness, but
Müller – who knew his medieval romances well and even began writing one
himself in 1815, a romance based on the life of the twelfth-century
troubadour Jaufré Rudel[3] – makes sure that the young man's every word
and action betrays it. But the miller is not a full-fledged rustic Rudel or
folkloric Tristan, any more than Müller is an unalloyed Romantic, and he
cannot sustain belief in two of the principal tenets of Romantic passion. In
the mythology of passionate love, death and self-awareness are in league,
and the sufferings of love are a privileged mode of understanding, a
spiritual branding that promises the artist a heightened knowledge of the
fire within, an enhancement of creativity. Müller's protagonist both parrots
the notion and disproves it by his inaction in 'Pause'. Furthermore, even
though passion culminates in the self-destruction of those who yield to it
with all their heart and soul, the true Romantic lover believes, by way of
compensation, in love's epiphany after death. Not so the miller –
pathetically, he attempts to console himself by repeating the credo of
fulfilment in the afterlife, but the effort fails somewhere in the interim
between 'Trock'ne Blumen' and 'Der Müller und der Bach'. The tragedy
is several shades blacker for it.

The poems

In 'Der Dichter, als Prolog', the Poet tells us that what follows is merely a diversion in the latest style intended for our amusement. This is art, not life; if the moonlight breaks out from a melancholy cluster of clouds, why, it is literary fashion to do so. Any stylistic rough edges are, he tells us tongue-in-cheek, deliberate evocations of *echt Deutsch* tradition. The poet who writes this ironically implies that he is of Shakespeare's company and has given us rustics for our amusement and *mille fleurs* tapestries for a stage set. A city sophisticate, a learned and self-conscious poet who lectures on Muses and artistic craft, mocks himself for having written of such country matters, and his readers are not invited to feel what the protagonist feels or care about his fate, only to admire the poet's skill in conjuring up a convincing landscape. Schubert had other intentions.

The cycle proper begins with 'Wanderschaft', which Schubert entitles 'Das Wandern'. I have retained Schubert's numbering; the poems he omitted are in their proper place in Müller's ordering and are numbered 6a, 15a, and 17a respectively.

1. Das Wandern (Wandering)

Das Wandern ist des Müllers Lust,
  Das Wandern!
    Das muß ein schlechter Müller sein,
Dem niemals fiel das Wandern ein,
  Das Wandern!

Vom Wasser haben wir's gelernt,
  Vom Wasser!
    Das hat nicht Rast bei Tag und
    Nacht,
Ist stets auf Wanderschaft bedacht,
  Das Wasser.

Das sehn wir auch den Rädern ab,
  Den Rädern!
    Die gar nicht gerne stille stehn,

Die sich mein Tag nicht müde drehn
  [gehn],
  Die Räder.

To wander is the miller's joy,
  To wander!
He must be a poor miller
who never thought of wandering,
  of wandering!

We have learned it from the water,
  from the water!
Day and night it does not rest,

but is always intent on wandering,
  the water!

We can see it in the wheels,
  the wheels!
They don't care at all for standing
  still,
they turn all day without tiring,

  the wheels.

Die Steine selbst, so schwer sie sind,	Even the stones, heavy as they are,
Die Steine!	the stones!
Sie tanzen mit den muntern Reihn	They join in the merry dance
Und wollen gar noch schneller sein,	and want to go even faster,
Die Steine.	the stones.
O Wandern, Wandern, meine Lust,	O wandering, wandering, my delight,
O wandern!	O wandering!
Herr Meister und Frau Meisterin,	Master and mistress, let me go
Laßt mich in Frieden weiter ziehn	on my way in peace
Und wandern.	and go wandering.

The sole human speaker in this monodrama is a miller who wishes to leave his present place of employment – a gentle, goodhearted creature, he asks his master and mistress for permission – and go wandering. Implicit in his song is his belief that only to those who roam are the beauty of life and the secrets of the world revealed. Humankind and Nature alike are beset by *Fernweh*, that eloquent German literalism that bespeaks the opposite of *Heimweh*, or homesickness. So innate is the urge to go forth on a journey that the very stones, nature's most permanent and immobile element, move as the millstones grind the grain; anthropomorphized as unlikely candidates for *Wanderlust*, they wish they could dance still faster. The assertion comes from the annals of Romanticism, in particular, its desire to animate the universe, and is clothed in the garb of folksong, the key words further emphasized by the single-iambic refrains. Alan Cottrell points to the transformation of the refrain in each stanza and its placement after first one and then after two lines; both features impart a forward stride to the movement, mitigate monotony, and rhythmically enliven the poem.[4] But the Romantic credos the miller utters in this poem are as much an expression of the desire to believe as of belief itself. The miller attempts to forge an identity for himself: 'Wandering is a (Romantic) miller's joy, therefore, I shall be a true miller and wander', but he is not already a wanderer, like the alienated *viator* of *Die Winterreise*. Rather, he feels he should *become* one.

2. Wohin? (Where to?)

Ich hört' ein Bächlein rauschen	I heard a little brook
Wohl aus dem Felsenquell,	babbling from its rocky source,
Hinab zum Tale rauschen	babbling down to the valley,
So frisch und wunderhell.	so bright and wondrously clear.

Ich weiß nicht, wie mir wurde,	I know not what came over me,
Nicht, wer den Rat mir gab,	nor who gave me the idea.
Ich mußte gleich [auch] hinunter	I had to go down there too,
Mit meinem Wanderstab.	with my wanderer's staff.
Hinunter und immer weiter,	Downward and ever onwards,
Und immer dem Bache nach,	and always following the brook,
Und immer frischer rauschte,	and the brook babbled on, ever brighter
Und immer heller der Bach.	and ever clearer.
Ist das denn meine Straße?	Is this then my path?
O Bächlein, sprich, wohin?	O brook, tell me, where?
Du hast mit deinem Rauschen	With your babbling,
Mir ganz berauscht den Sinn.	you have quite bemused my mind.
Was sag ich denn von [vom] Rauschen?	Why do I speak of babbling?
Das kann kein Rauschen sein:	That cannot be babbling:
Es singen wohl die Nixen	it must be the water-sprites singing as
Dort unten ihren Reihn.	they dance their round-dance far below.
Laß singen, Gesell, laß rauschen,	Let the singing and babbling go on, lad,
Und wandre fröhlich nach!	let it babble and follow merrily along!
Es gehn ja Mühlenräder	There are mill-wheels turning
In jedem klaren Bach.	in every clear brook.

Müller may have adapted the opening line of this poem and the motif of the rushing brook as a guide for wanderers from Clemens Brentano's 'Ich hört' ein Sichlein rauschen' in *Des Knaben Wunderhorn*, especially the first and last (fifth) stanzas:

Ich hört' ein Sichlein rauschen,	I heard a scythe rustling
Wohl rauschen durch das Korn,	through the cornfield,
Ich hört' ein Mägdlein klagen,	I heard a maiden who had
Sie hätt' ihr Lieb verlorn.	lost her sweetheart lamenting.
. . .	
Laß rauschen, Lieb, laß rauschen,	Let it babble, love, let it babble.
Ich weiß nicht, wie mir wird,	I do not know what will become of me.
Die Bächlein immer rauschen,	The little brooks always babble
Und keines sich verirrt.[5]	and not one of them goes astray.

Müller knew both the poet and the anthology well. In his diary for 31 October 1815, he writes of lending his own copy of *Des Knaben Wunderhorn* to a young man who had attempted to find it at the lending library and could not.[6] Readers who knew the earlier poem might even have heard in Müller's work a foreshadowing of the unrequited love to come.

In folksong and Romantic poetry, Nature is an enchantress who compels those who hear its voice to do its bidding, the imperatives it issues all the more powerful because its language is one that human listeners cannot understand. The source of the rushing water is mysterious (a 'Felsen-quell'), while the adjective 'wunderhell' and the threefold 'and' of stanza 3 reflect something of the enchanted, dream-like fluidity of unknown depths beyond human speech. Like the water, the poem flows along stream-like, as when the word 'hinunter' from stanza 2 is picked up in stanza 3 and then carried forward. The miller knows the Teutonic water myths of sirens on the Rhine, nixies, and water sprites, their erotic allure and their covert threat of death in the depths. This is the first enticement to become one with Nature, a Romantic unity possible only in death; the word 'hinunter' is an ominous foreshadowing of the youth's death 'down under' the surface of the brook, which magically swells from a 'Bächlein', a cosy little brook, to a 'Bach' at the first hint of Nature's power. The miller wonders whether the brook represents Destiny's guidance, a force all the more inscrutable because its metaphor, water, is clear: 'Ist das denn meine Straße?' The water-music threatens to flood his consciousness with enchantment, but at the end, he shakes off its spell and goes on in search – of a job. 'Wohin?' is not a question a true Romantic voyager would ask. *Sehnsucht* or longing, the nameless yearning that impels Eichendorff's or Novalis's poetic personae out into the unbounded world with no thought of a destination, is not what impels Müller's miller, who plans to stop at the next mill. And yet, Müller cleverly leaves the source of the directive 'Laß singen, Gesell, laß rauschen, / und wandre fröhlich nach' at the end unclear. Do the water-sprites (the brook as the voice of Destiny) bid him travel onwards to the mill, or is the youth talking to himself?

Already in the next song, the motion stops, although the lad is unsure whether to continue travelling or to stay at the mill he finds.

3. Halt! (Stop!)

Eine Mühle seh' ich blicken [blinken]	I see a mill gleaming
Aus den Erlen heraus,	among the alders,
Durch Rauschen und Singen	The roar of the mill-wheels
Bricht Rädergebraus.	breaks through the babbling and singing.

Ei willkommen, ei willkommen,	Now welcome, welcome,
Süßer Mühlengesang!	sweet mill-song!
Und das Haus, wie so traulich!	And how inviting the house is!
Und die Fenster, wie blank!	How brightly the windows gleam!
Und die Sonne, wie helle	And how brightly the sun
Vom Himmel sie scheint!	shines in the sky!
Ei, Bächlein, liebes Bächlein,	Now brook, dear little brook,
War es also gemeint?	is this what you meant?

Müller would surely have known Eichendorff's poem 'Frühlingsfahrt' (Springtime journey), first published in a literary periodical for 1818 that included some of his own miller-poems in their early incarnation. Of the 'two hale and hearty young fellows' in Eichendorff's poem, one chooses a Philistine burgher's existence, complete with wife, work, and child, while the other is a singer, a wandering poet who listens to the enticing voices of the sirens. In one reading of the poem, the two fellows are emblematic of conflicting desires within the Romantic self, desires both to roam beyond one's limits and to put down roots. Müller's 'Halt!' exemplifies the same conflict, but the two competing psychic forces are no longer of equivalent strength. The heart of a vagabond does not beat in the miller's breast – quite the contrary. The 'sweet mill-song' he greets with such enthusiasm (the exclamation point in the title is eloquent) is not the song of the nixies, but the song of domesticity and daylight. For the poet-miller, everything sings; even the 'Gebraus' or noise of the mill-wheels soon becomes 'Gesang'. The sun shines in the pristine windows and tells the youth that here is cleanliness and the work-ethic. (The 'Fenster wie blank' are a recurrent image in Müller's poetry, the young woman's window an opening which enables the lovers to see one another while separating them by an invisible barrier.) And yet, he is unsure whether he should stop and asks the brook, 'Was this what you meant?' The bright sun beckons him onwards, and the mill invites him inside; he must choose between the attractions of journeying and the haven of the mill. In the next poem, we discover that he has chosen the latter.

4. Danksagung an den Bach (Song of thanks to the brook)

War es also gemeint,	Is this what you meant,
Mein rauschender Freund,	my babbling friend?
Dein Singen, dein Klingen,	Your singing, your murmuring,
War es also gemeint?	is this what you meant?

'Zur Müllerin hin!'	'Go to the miller maid!'
So lautet der Sinn.	This is your meaning.
Gelt, hab ich's verstanden?	Have I understood you?
'Zur Müllerin hin!'	Go to the miller maid!
Hat *sie* dich geschickt?	Did she send you?
Oder hast mich berückt?	Or did you enchant me?
Das möcht' ich noch wissen,	I'd like to know this as well:
Ob *sie* dich geschickt.	if she sent you.
Nun wie's auch mag sein,	Well, however it may be,
Ich gebe mich drein:	I submit to my fate.
Was ich such', ist gefunden,	I've found what I sought,
Wie's immer mag sein.	however it may be.
Nach Arbeit ich frug,	I wanted work,
Nun hab' ich genug,	and now I have enough
Für die Hände, für's Herze	for the hands, for the heart,
Vollauf genug!	enough and more!

Müller links 'Halt!' and 'Danksagung an den Bach' when he has the youth ask the same question, 'War es also gemeint?', in close proximity. The youth, who has seen the miller maid in the meantime, now tries to persuade himself that his arrival at the mill is destined, that the brook is her emissary sent to fetch him. The single word 'Gelt' (really, truly) at the beginning of the line, suggestive of naturalistic speech rather than poetic diction – a separate accented monosyllabic foot unto itself – is uncertainty and assertion simultaneously. The miller, who is not analytically inclined, does not pursue the question any more, but declares himself content, having found what he sought. A true Romantic, Madeleine Haefeli-Rasi suggests, would not say 'gefunden' so early in life.[7]

Müller has been accused of poor rhymes, and the first three stanzas would seem to bear this out. However, the rhyming couplets in lines 1 and 2 are notably strong and regular in the final two stanzas when the miller sets aside his uncertainty. Perhaps inexact rhymes are the indices of anxious query and the rhymes put back in order at the end are the register of momentary contentment.

5. Am Feierabend (When the day's work is done)

Hätt' ich tausend	If only I had a thousand
Arme zu rühren!	arms to wield!
Könnt' ich brausend	If only I could drive
Die Räder führen!	the rushing wheels!
Könnt' ich wehen	If only I could blow
Durch alle Haine!	through all the woods,
Könnt' ich drehen	if only I could turn
Alle Steine!	all the mill-stones
Daß die schöne Müllerin	so that the beautiful miller maid
Merkte meinen treuen Sinn!	would see my true love!
Ach, wie ist mein Arm so schwach!	Oh, how weak my arms are!
Was ich hebe, was ich trage,	What I can lift, what I can carry,
Was ich schneide, was ich schlage,	what I can cut, what I can hammer,
Jeder Knappe tut es [mir's] nach.	any apprentice can do too.
Und da sitz' ich in der großen Runde,	And there I sit with them in a circle,
Zu der stillen kühlen Feierstunde,	in the quiet, cool leisure hour,
Und der Meister spricht [sagt] zu	and the master says to us all:
allen:	
'Euer Werk hat mir gefallen';	'I am pleased with your work.'
Und das liebe Mädchen sagt	And the dear maiden
Allen eine gute Nacht.	bids us all goodnight.

The miller is torn by conflict between a surge of desperate desire and the advent of night on the one hand and his master's daylight and duty-bound satisfaction in work well done on the other. In the ten lines of stanza 1, boundaries the lad himself has set become intolerable, and a flood of wishes well up from within, the stream of subjunctives 'Hätt' ... Könnt' ... Könnt' ...Könnt'' a desperate fourfold impulsion into the world of change and motion. The clipped, breathless trochaic dimeters (trochees are less common than iambs in German verse, and the accented initial syllable is an index of forcefulness); the multiple exclamation points; the occasional addition of dactyls to the trochees for a more rapid poetic rhythm are all registers of a floodtide of feeling. But the energy of the beginning ebbs away altogether in the space between stanzas 1 and 2. There is massive resignation in the single word 'Ach', and the lines 'relax' from dimeters to tetrameters and even pentameters for lines 5 and 6, the designation of evening leisure. The commonplace male fantasy of heroic physical exploits to attract a woman's attention is, he realizes, an impossibility, and the disparity between dream and reality is measured in the ironic parallelisms of the words 'Was ich hebe, was ich trage, / was ich schneide, was ich schlage', each verb an additional index of incapacity. Yet desire is still evident in the phrase 'das liebe Mädchen' rather than 'die schöne Müllerin'. The latter designation would have placed her within her father's sphere of work and duty, while the former is the lad's attempt to accomplish in wish-fulfilment what is not happening in reality: to draw her from her father's side to his. Similarly, the word 'all' has two different connotations in the second stanza, registered in the differing placement of the word. The master says goodnight to all in the literal world of observed fact and at the end of the poetic line; as rhyme is a primary ordering principle in rhyming verse, it is tempting to interpret the word 'allen' as indicative of the father's world of order. When the miller maid says goodnight to all, the word 'allen' appears at the beginning of the last line, and the emphatic initial trochee has a heightened emotional intensity. The miller says 'all' and, in his longing, means 'one/me', and both meanings are implicit in the line.

6. Der Neugierige (The inquisitive one)

Ich frage keine Blume,	I ask no flower,
Ich frage keinen Stern,	I ask no star.
Sie können mir nicht sagen,	None of them can tell me
Was ich erführ' so gern.	what I so greatly want to hear.
Ich bin ja auch kein Gärtner,	I am, after all, no gardener,
Die Sterne stehn zu hoch;	and the stars are too high.
Mein Bächlein will ich fragen,	I will ask my brook
Ob mich mein Herz belog.	whether my heart has lied to me.
O Bächlein meiner Liebe,	O little brook of my love,
Wie bist du heut so stumm!	how silent you are today!
Will ja nur eines wissen,	I want to know just one thing,
Ein Wörtchen um und um.	one little word, over and over again.
'Ja', heißt das eine Wörtchen,	One word is Yes,
Das andre heißet 'Nein',	the other is No.
Die beiden Wörtchen schließen	The two little words contain
Die ganze Welt mir ein.	the whole world for me.
O Bächlein meiner Liebe,	O little brook of my love,
Was bist du wunderlich!	how strange you are today!
Will's ja nicht weiter sagen,	I'll tell no one else:
Sag', Bächlein, liebt sie mich?	tell me, little brook, does she love me?

The youth pins his entire hopes for existence on the possibility of the word 'Yes', on reciprocity in love, but cannot help thinking of the word 'No' at the same time. The tragic price of consciousness in Müller's poetic world is the oppositional nature of reality, signified by the polarities that cluster thick and fast in his verse. 'Ja', one notices, is placed at the beginning of the line and occupies a poetic foot unto itself, in unmistakable emphasis, while 'Nein' is placed at the *end* of the line.

The key word of the poem is 'stumm'. In vain the miller hopes that Nature, the fountainhead of all wisdom, will reveal her secret to him, but he cannot understand what it says to him. In the lad's entreaties in stanzas 1 and 2 is the assumption that only Nature knows the inmost workings of his heart and the truth of what transpires at the mill. Nature to post-Romantic poets is a puzzle, a problem to be investigated in different realms of specialization (gardener-botanist, astronomer, and so on), hence the miller's rejection of a possible answer from the flowers and the heavens; as a miller who works by the water, he will ask the brook. The adjective 'wunderlich' or 'odd, strange' recurs often in Müller's verse to signify a certain eerie power, beyond comprehension: the crow and the hurdy-gurdy player in *Die Winterreise* are both described this way. But the brook remains 'mute', incomprehensible to him. The poem ends with the miller asserting that *he* will say no more and demanding that the brook answer his direct question, 'Sag', Bächlein, liebt sie mich?', the imperative stressed at the beginning of the line. Tellingly, there is no answer, but Schubert understood the miller's desire for the 'little word Yes' when he ends with tonic closure in the vocal line, not a questioning inflection but tonal certainty.

Müller published an earlier version of 'Der Neugierige' in *Der Gesellschafter* for 6 June 1818, the second stanza more stilted – especially the last line, 'Ich hoff', es heißt nicht: "Nein!"' (I hope it isn't No) – than the final version in the *Waldhornisten-Gedichte I*. Not until after this version did Müller change 'still' in line 2 to the more allusive 'stumm'.

6a. Das Mühlenleben (Life at the mill) – the first of the poems that Schubert omitted from the narrative

The idealization of the miller's daughter is the subject of this poem – a re-working of chivalric love in costumes from a later day. Müller, who translated Minnesinger poetry from the Manesse Codex, turns her into a quasi-divine medieval *Herrin*, likened to the omnipotent gaze of God. The transforming power she exercises on the miller's emotions is expressed through the reversal of his reaction to the sound of the mill-wheel. In stanzas 3 and 4, the sound is oppressive, and he wants to escape into the open air to be with her. Once he has seen her, the same sounds become dance music, like the stones and mill-wheels of 'Das Wandern'. The sight of her as she moves about, praising and gently chastising the mill workers, has the effect of poeticizing the young miller's world, making it 'worthy of song'. This is love as the wish for limits and certainty, for a workaday world graced and regulated by its own in-house saint. As in Minnesinger verse, the miller's daughter is depicted as a civilizing force.

We can only guess why Schubert 'found nothing of music' in the poems he omitted from the body of *Die schöne Müllerin*. 'Das Mühlenleben', all ten quatrains of it, is longer than most of the other poems in the cycle, but length alone would not necessarily have been a factor had the contents pleased him more. I wonder if he perhaps found the depiction of the miller maid in 'Das Mühlenleben' as part plaster-of-Paris saint, part lordly lady, less effective than the idealization that flourishes best in absence. Where the miller maid herself is not present on the scene, the youth can more easily exult in a lover's feverish longing. Schubert, by excising this poem, limits the miller maid's appearances to a few significantly brief lines and thereby suggests more strongly that the miller's love is almost entirely the product of his own longing, with little nourishment in reality.

7. Ungeduld (Impatience)

Ich schnitt' es gern in alle Rinden ein,	I would like to carve it in the bark of every tree,
Ich grüb' es gern in jeden Kieselstein,	I'd like to engrave it on every pebble.
Ich möcht' es sän auf jedes frische Beet	I want to sow it in every fresh plot of ground
Mit Kressensamen, der es schnell verrät,	with cress seeds that would quickly reveal it.
Auf jeden weißen Zettel möcht' ich's schreiben:	On every scrap of white paper I want to write it:
'Dein ist mein Herz, und soll es ewig bleiben'.	'My heart is yours and shall remain forever so!'
Ich möcht' mir ziehen einen jungen Star,	I would like to train a young starling
Bis daß er spräch' die Worte rein und klar,	till it could speak the words pure and clear,
Bis er sie spräch' mit meines Mundes Klang,	till it spoke them with the sound of my voice,

Mit meines Herzens vollem, heißem
  Drang;
Dann säng' er hell durch ihre
  Fensterscheiben:
'Dein ist mein Herz, und soll es ewig
  bleiben'.

with my heart's full, ardent yearning.
Then it would sing brightly at her
  window:
Thine is my heart and shall forever
  remain so!

Den Morgenwinden möcht' ich's
  hauchen ein,
Ich möcht' es säuseln durch den regen
  Hain;
O, leuchtet' es aus jedem Blumenstern!
Trüg' es der Duft zu ihr von nah und
  fern!
Ihr Wogen, könnt' ihr nichts als Räder
  treiben?
Dein ist mein Herz, und soll es ewig
  bleiben!

I would like to breathe it to the
  morning wind,
I would like to whisper it through the
  budding grove.
Oh, if only it shone from every flower,
if fragrances could only waft it to her
  from far and near!
Waves, can you only drive
  mill-wheels?
Thine is my heart and shall remain so
  forever!

Ich meint', es müßt' in meinen Augen
  stehn,
Auf meinen Wangen müßt man's
  brennen sehn,
Zu lesen wär's auf meinem stummen
  Mund,
Ein jeder Atemzug gäb's laut ihr
  kund;
Und sie merkt nichts von all' dem
  bangen Treiben:
Dein ist mein Herz, und soll es ewig
  bleiben!

I should have thought it would show
  in my eyes,
could be seen burning on my cheeks,

could be read on my silent lips.

I should have thought my every breath
  would proclaim it to her.
And she takes no notice of all my
  anxious striving.
Thine is my heart and shall remain so
  forever!

Müller, who translated Marlowe's Faust drama and was well-read
in Elizabethan literature, modelled 'Ungeduld' on a passage from
Edmund Spenser's 'Colin Clouts come home again', first published in
1595:

> Her name in every tree I will endosse,
> That as the trees do grow, her name may grow:
> And in the ground each where will it engrosse,
> And fill with stones, that all men may it know.
> The speaking woods and murmuring waters fall,
> Her name Ile teach in knowen termes to frame:
> And eke my lambs, when for their dams they call,
> Ile teach to call for *Cynthia* by name.[8]

Looking at Spenser's poem, one realizes anew Müller's omission of any proper names from his Everyman–Everywoman tale. The miller wants all of Nature to proclaim, in human language *she* could understand, 'Thine is my heart', the word 'Dein' all the more emphatic for its placement at the beginning of the line and the rhythmic shift from iambs to this prolonged, accented monosyllabic foot. (Müller is adept at marking changes of tone, emphasis, address, and subject by means of rhythmic shifts.) The syntactical focus on her ownership, however unclaimed, of his heart is just one of many indices of the miller's frantic striving to force reciprocated love into being where it can only be given as a gift. The repetitive structure of the poem, the imagery, and the syntax all bespeak an insistent attempt to affix and fortify both the overt assertion that his heart belongs to her and the underlying frantic plea that she must therefore respond in kind. His fantasy of cutting the words 'Dein ist mein Herz' into trees and stones, of planting them in flowerbeds, is an archetypal siege of the unresponsive beloved, an imagined bombardment with the only weapons at a poet's disposal: words rhythmically arranged. One hears the heavy tread of unnaturally rhythmical iambic pentameters simultaneously as hammering on the closed door of the miller maid's heart and as a poetic clock whose ticking marks the passage of time, negating the eternal fidelity the miller wants so fervently ('und *soll* es ewig bleiben').

The poem is a study in the subjunctive mood. There are only two statements in the indicative in the entire poem: the refrain, which is only a positive assertion of a wish, and the crucial line, 'Und sie merkt nichts von all' dem bangen Treiben'. Müller's happy choice of the words 'bangen Treiben' makes apparent the fear that drives the seeming rapture. The Romantic's desire for a world that narcissistically mirrors the self is dashed on the rocks of his speechlessness and her ignorance of his feelings. Because he is mute in actuality, he imagines every empty surface or blank space as a writing tablet for words he dare not say aloud. Painfully aware of the gulf between his fervour and her indifference, the miller seems as if goading himself to speak to her in the next poem – but does he, or is this too a poetic script for words left unsaid?

8. Morgengruß (Morning greeting)

Guten Morgen, schöne Müllerin!	Good morning, lovely miller maid!
Wo steckst du gleich das Köpfchen hin,	Why do you quickly turn your head
Als wär' dir was geschehen?	away, as if something was wrong?
Verdrießt dich denn mein Gruß so schwer?	Does my greeting annoy you so much?
Verstört dich denn mein Blick so sehr?	Does my gaze upset you so much?
So muß ich wieder gehen.	Then I must go away again.
O laß mich nur von ferne stehn,	O let me just stand at a distance
Nach deinem lieben Fenster sehn,	and look at your dear window
Von ferne, ganz von ferne!	from far away, from quite far away!
Du blondes Köpfchen, komm hervor!	Come out, little blond head, come out!
Hervor aus eurem runden Tor,	Come out from your round gates,
Ihr blauen Morgensterne!	blue morning stars!
Ihr schlummertrunknen Äugelein,	Little eyes, drunk with sleep,
Ihr taubetrübten Blümelein,	little flowers, saddened by the dew,
Was scheuet ihr die Sonne?	why do you shrink from the sun?
Hat es die Nacht so gut gemeint,	Has the night been so good to you
Daß ihr euch schließt und bückt und weint	that you close yourself away and droop
Nach ihrer stillen Wonne?	and weep for its quiet bliss?
Nun schüttelt ab der Träume Flor,	Now shake off the veil of dreams
Und hebt euch frisch und frei empor	and rise up, refreshed and free,
In Gottes hellen Morgen!	to God's bright morning!
Die Lerche wirbelt in der Luft,	The lark is warbling in the sky,
Und aus dem tiefen Herzen ruft	and from deep within the heart,
Die Liebe Leid und Sorgen.	love calls out its pain and sorrow.

The language is revealing: one is not invited to envisage an actual encounter between the miller and miller maid.[9] Rather, the self-consciously poetic language and artificial metaphors bespeak a flight of fancy, an imagined scenario that takes place entirely within the miller's mind. The whole poem is written 'von ferne, ganz von ferne', distant from actuality. True feeling, spontaneous emotion, does not speak in phrases such as 'blaue Morgensterne', 'schlummertrunkene Äugelein', and 'taubetrübte Blümelein' ('taubetrübte' a neologism in place of 'taubenetzt'). The meaning of these polysyllabic flourishes goes beyond artifice to hints of tragic irony. 'Blue morning stars' is literally senseless as a metaphor for eyes, and Müller redoubles the disturbing effect by bidding them 'Come forth from your round gates'. The 'round gates' can only be interpreted physically and literally as the eye-sockets, a decidedly macabre association. Actually, 'hervor' comes from the preceding plea 'Du blondes Köpfchen, komm hervor', but the juxtaposition with 'ihr blauen Morgensterne' is unsettling. So too is the insistent metonymy – the miller maid is no more than a compilation of bodily fragments evocative of idealized feminine beauty. 'Flor' also has associations with the gauze or crape draperies of mourning. The verbal artifice is as yet unconnected with experience. When the miller ends his greeting with clichés of 'love's pain and sorrow', he lacks as yet any knowledge of the truth he invokes so blithely. 'Die Liebe Leid und Sorgen' are no more than words from which to fashion songs.

Once again, an element of Romanticism is invoked and then rejected. In the miller's imagination, his beloved has just passed a night of 'quiet wonder', a Romantic realm of mystic ecstasy she is reluctant to leave. Because she is a blank slate on which he writes his own desires and ideas, he imagines her as a poet like himself, but a poet still wedded to a time now over and done, fearful of the new sunlit world where he awaits his Luise-like beloved in 'God's bright morning'. Unlike the atheist-wanderer in *Die Winterreise*, the miller ostensibly believes in God, but he too finds no consolation, no possibility of transcendence, in religion.

9. Des Müllers Blumen (The miller's flowers)

Am Bach viel kleine Blumen stehn,
Aus hellen blauen Augen sehn;
Der Bach, der ist des Müllers Freund,
Und hellblau Liebchens Auge
  scheint,
Drum sind es meine Blumen.

Many little flowers grow by the brook,
and gaze from bright blue eyes.
The brook is the miller's friend,
and my sweetheart's eyes are bright
  blue,
therefore they are my flowers.

Dicht unter ihrem Fensterlein
Da pflanz ich meine Blumen ein,
[Da will ich pflanzen die Blumen ein,]
Da ruft ihr zu, wenn alles schweigt,
Wenn sich ihr Haupt zum Schlummer
  neigt,
Ihr wißt ja, was ich meine.

Right under her window
I will plant my flowers.

So call to her, when all is silent,
when she lays down her head to sleep

you know what I wish to say.

Und wenn sie tät die Äuglein zu,
Und schläft in süßer, süßer Ruh',
Dann lispelt als ein Traumgesicht
Ihr zu: 'Vergiß, vergiß mein nicht!'
Das ist es, was ich meine.

And when she closes her eyes
and sleeps in sweet, sweet repose,
then whisper to her as if in a dream:
forget, forget-me-not!
That's what I wish to say.

Und schließt sie früh die Laden auf,	And when she opens the shutters early
Dann schaut mit Liebesblick hinauf:	in the morning, then gaze up at her
Der Tau in euren Äugelein,	lovingly; the dew in your eyes
Das sollen meine Tränen sein,	shall be my tears
Die will ich auf euch weinen.	that I shed upon you.

Stanza 2, possibly the entire poem, could have been written in response to Luise Hensel's gardener courtship poems from the *Liederspiel*.

Comparison of a sweetheart's eyes to blue flowers is a cliché of love poetry, but in 'Des Müllers Blumen', Müller varies the formula. The miller comes close to fusing the little blue flowers with his beloved's eyes and actually does so in 'Tränenregen', linked to 'Des Müllers Blumen' as well by the tears imagined in this poem and shed in the next. Once again, he seeks a Romantic alliance with Nature in which the symbiotic relationship of the brook and its flowers signifies the intimacy he desires with the miller maid; once again, the flowers/Nature are directed to convey symbolic messages that he himself, mute in her presence, cannot say. Strikingly, the flowers are identified both with the maiden and with the miller, as nocturnal messengers who convey subliminal messages for him and metonymic symbols of her. This is a vision of love as fused identities, the boundaries between selves blurred.

'Des Müllers Blumen' foreshadows 'Mein!' in its unfounded assertions of possession. Here, however, the miller lays claim to the miller's daughter only very circuitously, shy of an outright statement that she is his. Instead, he proclaims that the *flowers*, 'hellblau' like her eyes, are his. The somewhat muddled syntax of the first stanza, especially in lines 3–5, is not ineptitude on Müller's part but psychologically revealing language, its indirections and coyness the signifiers of the miller's cloudy logic as he constructs his illusions of reciprocated love. What is the connection between 'the brook that is the miller's friend' in line 3 and the fourth line to which it is grammatically joined ('and my sweetheart's eyes are bright blue')? One notices that the couplet does not rhyme, is not even assonant, and that the miller refers to himself in the third person, saying 'the miller's friend' rather than '*my* friend'. In this roundabout fashion, he hints that the brook should be his go-between because they are kindred spirits equally devoted to bright blue eyes, that the flowers/eyes are therefore his.

Müller underscores the sidelong assertions of ownership in the five-line stanzaic form in which the fifth line is 'odd man out' each time, following after two more or less rhymed couplets. Because of this, the line sounds like a truncated couplet, more forceful, even abrupt in its effect, emphasizing the claim 'Drum sind es meine Blumen'. Even though the final line ends either with the penultimate -ei diphthong that chimes throughout the poem or with a word from earlier in the stanza ('Blumen'), it does not rhyme with what comes before, and that too makes it stand out. At the end of stanzas 2 and 3, one even hears in the verb 'meinen' (to mean, intend, think, believe) the linguistic echo of the possessive to which the miller has no claim in reality. Schubert, one notices, repeats the last line of the poem in masterful compensation for what is lost from poetic form in musical setting. Music turns all poetry into prose, and therefore the effect of the truncated ending of each stanza cannot be duplicated in song. Recognizing the strategy of self-deception at the heart of the poem, Schubert ends the first invocation of the phrase with deceptive harmonic motion and non-tonic closure in the vocal line. His miller must then repeat the same words to a more definitive ending in order to present illusion as fact.

The fourth line of stanza 3, with its injunction 'Vergiß, vergiß mein nicht', is usually translated as if the Freudian stammer were not there, as if the initial invocation of 'Vergiß' were poetic filler to complete the line in tetrameters. But I believe Müller had more in mind for the folk-like repetition – another instance of his favourite play of opposites ('Forget, forget me not') – than that. The miller fears that the maiden can, and does, forget him easily because he is of little or no importance to her. His fear comes irresistibly to the surface, even in the context of this daydream whose contours are cut and moulded to his desire, in the form of a revealing stutter. The truer verb 'forget', one notices, appears first.

10. Tränenregen (Shower of tears)

Wir saßen so traulich beisammen	We sat together in such closeness
Im kühlen Erlendach,	beneath the cool canopy of the alders.
Wir schauten so traulich zusammen	We looked down together in such
Hinab in den rieselnden Bach.	intimacy into the rippling brook.
Der Mond war auch gekommen,	And the moon came too,
Die Sternlein hinterdrein,	and after it the stars,
Und schauten so traulich zusammen	and gazed down so harmoniously
In den silbernen Spiegel hinein.	into the silver mirror.
Ich sah nach keinem Monde,	I did not look at the moon
Nach keinem Sternenschein,	or the stars.
Ich schaute nach ihrem Bilde,	I looked at her reflection,
Nach ihren Augen [ihrem Auge]	at her eyes alone.
allein.	

Und sahe sie nicken und blicken
Herauf aus dem seligen Bach,
Die Blümlein am Ufer, die blauen,
Sie nickten und blickten ihr nach.

And saw them nod and gaze up
from the happy brook;
the flowers on the bank, the blue ones,
nodded and gazed at her.

Und in den Bach versunken
Der ganze Himmel schien,
Und wollte mich mit hinunter
In seine Tiefe ziehn.

And the whole sky seemed to be
submerged in the brook
and wanted to draw me down
into its depths.

Und über den Wolken und Sternen
Da rieselte munter der Bach,
Und rief mit Singen und Klingen:

And the brook rippled happily
over the clouds and the stars
and called with its singing and
ringing:

'Geselle, Geselle, mir nach!'

'Friend, friend, follow me!'

Da gingen die Augen mir über,
Da ward es im Spiegel so kraus;
Sie sprach: 'Es kommt ein Regen,
Ade, ich geh' nach Haus'.

Then my eyes filled with tears,
and the mirror was blurred.
She said, 'It's about to rain.
Good-bye. I'm going home.'

The miller's longing for *Traulichkeit* (trusting, cosy intimacy, a word with multiple connotations of marriage) is the subject of the first two stanzas, with their insistent rhymes of 'beisammen' and 'zusammen'. The moon and stars are the heavenly coordinates of the miller and miller maid; the advent of night should bring everything 'so traulich zusammen', humankind and Nature fused in love. The miller knows what true Romantic *Traulichkeit* would be when he speaks of the beloved's eyes as divorced from her body, 'winking and blinking' from within the brook, although one notes as well that he sees an unattainable reflection, not the real person. But the miller maid only sits next to him, not with him in true trust and intimacy, and the twilight fantasy of shared closeness is just that: a fantasy. For the first and only time in the cycle, the two are alone together, but they say nothing. The miller fills the unbridgeable distance between them with visions of the heavens themselves contained within the watery, erotic element that symbolizes Death – as in the Narcissus myth, the miller both sees his own reflection and stares into the face of death. The cosmos and consciousness alike turn inside out and upside down, the brook rushing *over* the stars and moon contained within it in a magical world of reflected images, a world in which the nixies sing again. But with the youth's tears and the maiden's banal and unromantic words of departure, cosmic magic and its temptations vanish, and prosy reality returns. It is here, as John Reed points out, that we remember how much Heine, who perfected the art of deflating lofty sentiments in the last line or two of a poem

(*Stimmungsbrechung*), respected Müller.[10] The seventh stanza is, one notices, a solitary entity, unlike the paired stanzas that precede it (stanzas 1 and 2 linked by the togetherness both of the couple and the cosmos, stanzas 3 and 4 by images of sight and seeing, stanzas 5 and 6 by the cosmic dissolution of forms). The miller maid's words are all the more stark because of their unadorned iambic rhythms, the curtness in harsh contrast with the miller's anapaests in lines 1 and 2. At her words of departure, the poem ends, without reproach, in a silence filled with denial of the true import of what she has just said and done.

In both of the Schubert–Müller cycles, Nature invites the protagonist to become one with it, a feat only possible in death. In 'Der Lindenbaum', the fifth song of *Die Winterreise*, the wanderer remembers the sound of linden leaves rustling as if calling to him, 'Come here to me, lad, here you will find your rest!' The invitation is a beckoning to death: if the wanderer in the midst of a winter storm continues to stand, listening raptly to the voices within his mind, he will freeze and die. The miller's fantasy that the brook wants to draw him within its depths is a prophetic fancy, a temptation to which he succumbs at the end. In the following poem, 'Mein!', the youth begins his song of rejoicing with the command that the brook stop its rustling noise: 'Bächlein, laß dein Rauschen sein'. He wants all other sounds to cease so that he might proclaim and all might hear that the lovely miller maid is his, but he also dismisses for the moment the brook's invitation to submerge himself in its depths.

11. Mein! (Mine!)

Bächlein, laß dein Rauschen sein!	Brook, stop your babbling!
Räder, stellt eu'r Brausen ein!	Mill-wheels, cease your roaring!
All ihr muntern Waldvögelein,	All you merry little forest birds,
Groß und klein,	large and small,
Endet eure Melodein!	end your warbling!
Durch den Hain	Throughout the woods,
Aus und ein	within and beyond,
Schalle heut' *ein* Reim allein:	let one rhyme alone ring out today:
Die geliebte Müllerin ist *mein*!	the beloved miller-maid is mine!
Mein!	Mine!
Frühling, sind das alle deine	Spring, are those all the flowers you
Blümelein?	have?
Sonne, hast du keinen hellern Schein?	Sun, have you no brighter light?
Ach, so muß ich ganz allein,	Ah, then I must remain all alone
Mit dem seligen Worte *mein*,	with this blissful word of mine,
Unverstanden in der weiten	uncomprehended anywhere in the
Schöpfung sein!	wide world!

Either the miller's triumphal claim of possession is a delusion or the miller maid has bestowed some unknown kindness on the lad to produce this outburst of joy. One can fantasize a sweetly apologetic smile the morning after 'Tränenregen', but Müller says nothing. The omission of any hint of reciprocated love between 'Tränenregen', which indeed ends with evidence to the contrary, and 'Mein!' is surely among the most significant omissions of the entire narrative.

Here, the refrain of 'Ungeduld' – 'Dein ist mein Herz, und soll es ewig bleiben' – contracts to the single word 'Mein!' All of the trochaic lines (more emphatic than iambs) rhyme on the syllable '-ein'; it even appears as the central word in the central line of the poem, where it is italicized: 'Schalle heut' *ein* Reim allein'. In 'Der Neugierige', the poet had implored the stream to say the one word he wishes to hear: 'Will ja nur Eines wissen, / *Ein* Wörtchen um und um'. Now the italicized indefinite article of that question returns in the poem which brings the answer, a climactic moment in the cycle. In Müller's cycle, it is twelfth of twenty-three poems, that is, exactly central, with eleven poems on either side.

'Mein!' is similar to 'Am Feierabend' in its psychological fever chart. In each, a heaven-storming surge of emotional current collapses by the poem's end, the defeat signalled by the exhausted exclamation 'Ach'. He can neither maintain the illusion that she belongs to him for the duration of a single poem nor give it up. Müller chooses his words precisely, the result a classic case of hedging: the miller declares, not that he is all alone, but that he must go forth all alone with the *word* 'Mein!' – the word only, not what it signifies. Almost rent asunder by the conflict, he wildly proposes venturing forth into 'the wide world' like a vagabond out of Eichendorff, a Romantic actor's remedy for a post-Romantic soul and one he does not take. Julius Stockhausen was so struck by the vacillation between over-confidence and doubt in 'Mein!' that he described the song in his diary for 1862 as 'truly insanity' ('Das ist ein wahres Rasen').[11]

Those familiar with Schubert's song might not realize until they read the printed poem what a complex formal structure it is: a single fifteen-line stanza in which the line lengths change often and drastically, ranging from a line with a single syllable to a final hexameter line that unfurls to eleven syllables, wide creation symbolized in the expanse beyond previous limits. With the exclamation 'Ach', the breathless, shorter lines give way to longer, slower lines, but still changeable in length. The control exercised by the single rhyme-sound and the insistent trochees is in conflict throughout with the calculated unpredictability of the larger phrase rhythms, the register of a mind disordered.

12. Pause

Meine Laute hab' ich gehängt an die Wand,	I have hung my lute on the wall
Hab' sie umschlungen mit einem grünen Band –	and tied a green ribbon around it.
Ich kann nicht mehr singen, mein Herz ist zu voll,	I can no longer sing; my heart is too full.
Weiß nicht, wie ich's in Reime zwingen soll.	I don't know how to force it into rhyme.
Meiner Sehnsucht allerheißesten Schmerz	I could express the most ardent
Durft' ich aushauchen in Liederscherz [Liederschmerz],	pangs of my longing in sorrowful song,
Und wie ich klagte so süss und fein,	and when I lamented so sweetly and delicately,
Meint' [Glaubt'] ich doch, mein Leiden wär' nicht klein.	I thought then my sorrow was not trifling.
Ei, wie groß ist wohl meines Glückes Last,	Oh, is the burden of my happiness so great
Daß kein Klang auf Erden es in sich faßt?	that no sound on earth can express it?
Nun, liebe Laute, ruh' an dem Nagel hier!	Now, dear lute, rest here on the nail!
Und weht ein Lüftchen über die Saiten dir,	If a breath of air sweeps over your strings,
Und streift eine Biene mit ihren Flügeln dich,	or a bee brushes you with its wings,
Da wird mir [mir so] bange und es durchschauert mich.	I shall be afraid and shiver!
Warum ließ ich das Band auch hängen so lang?	Why have I left the ribbon hanging down so far?
Oft fliegt's um die Saiten mit seufzendem Klang.	Often it flutters across the strings with a sighing sound.
Ist es der Nachklang meiner Liebespein?	Is that the echo of love's sorrow?
Soll es das Vorspiel neuer Lieder sein?	Could it be the prelude to new songs?

This is literally a pause in the cycle, a hiatus between the highest peak of the narrative and its subsequent descent to tragedy and death. The long four- and five-beat lines can only be read slowly, checking the breathless impetus of 'Mein!'. Here, the miller identifies himself belatedly as a poet-singer, but one trapped in a creative block, a pause between poems and poetic insights. 'Pause' is thus a sophisticated paradox: a poem fashioned from the inability – actually, the refusal – to write new poems and sing new songs because the poet cannot bear the truth that is the only possible subject of those songs. Notably, Müller writes of 'Lieder*s*cherz,' or 'jesting song', but Schubert alters the word to 'Liedersch*m*erz'. The poet's miller expresses sorrow through its opposite mode, while the composer's miller makes a more direct equation between emotional experience and the art distilled from it.

A sketch of Müller's aesthetic of poetry peers through the lines of 'Pause'. Poetry, in his view, requires all of one's conscious will, unperturbed by emotional distress. When a poet's inner balance is gone, the instrument by which poetry is expressed is left hanging, no longer played by a rational artist in full command of his powers but by a whim of nature. The result is eerie, shapeless music – a 'sighing lament'. The wavering poetic metres are perhaps Müller's index of poetry in abeyance, its creator lacking the disciplined focus required to maintain a consistent rhythmic form: lines 1 and 2 are trochaic pentameters with a mixture of dactyls, line 3 consists of iambic and anapaestic tetrameters, its paired line 4 reverts back to trochees, and so on. The very syntax bespeaks powerlessness. When the miller says, 'Da wird *mir* bange und es durchschauert *mich*' (italics mine), the dative and accusative personal pronouns enforce the sense that he feels himself acted upon rather than acting himself, that he has lost the power of volition and is being inexorably impelled towards a destiny he dreads.

Above all, this is a poem of unsuccessful denial. The miller's previous poems have been inspired by love's sorrow; when he asks at the end if this hiatus is the prelude to new songs, he betrays his underlying fear of impending tragedy. He can neither admit his dread directly nor banish it from his thoughts, and the more he says, the closer he comes to admission in spite of himself. When he comes too close, he falls silent, and the poem ends.

4

Disillusionment and death: the poetic texts continued

'Pause' forms a natural break in the cycle before the stage darkens and the tale turns tragic. The tragedy begins with the hunter already present and the miller maid obliquely announcing her infatuation with him. The miller, however, does not yet see the truth and continues to interpret her words in accord with his own longing.

13. Mit dem grünen Lautenbande (With the green lute ribbon)

'Schad' um das schöne grüne Band,

Daß es verbleicht hier an der Wand,
Ich hab' das Grün so gern!'
So sprachst du, Liebchen, heut' zu
    mir;
Gleich knüpf' ich's ab und send' es dir:
Nun hab' das Grüne gern!

Ich auch dein ganzer Liebster weiß,
Soll Grün doch haben seinen Preis,
Und ich auch hab' es gern.
Weil unsre Lieb ist immer grün
Weil grün der Hoffnung Fernen
    blühn,
Drum haben wir es gern.

Nun schlingst du [schlinge] in die
    Locken dein
Das grüne Band gefällig ein,
Du hast ja's Grün so gern.
Dann weiß ich, wo die Hoffnung
    wohnt [grünt]
Dann weiß ich, wo die Liebe thront,
Dann hab' ich's Grün erst gern.

'What a pity that the pretty green
    ribbon
should fade on the wall here –
I am so fond of green!'
You said that to me today, sweetheart:

I untied the ribbon at once and sent it.
Now delight in green!

Even if your beloved is all in white,
green can still have its reward,
and I am fond of it too.
For our love is evergreen,
for distant hope blossoms green,

that's why we are fond of it.

Now tie the green ribbon

prettily in your hair.
You are so fond of green.
Then I shall know where hope lives,

then I shall know where love reigns.
Then I shall truly delight in green.

For the second and last time, the miller maid speaks to the miller. Her seemingly inconsequential remark signifies that she has already met the hunter, her attraction to the colour green emblematic of her attraction to him. Green garb for those who live in the green woods is a common motif in folk poetry and the fake-folk progeny of educated poets: the Teutonized Italian maiden of Hugo Wolf's 'Gesegnet sei das Grün und wer es trägt' (Blessed be green and he who wears it) in the *Italienisches Liederbuch* by Paul Heyse (*Italian Songbook*, a collection of Italian folk poems translated into German by Heyse and published in 1860) proclaims, 'In Grün sich kleiden ist der Jäger Brauch, / Ein grünes Kleid trägt mein Geliebter auch' (It is the hunter's custom to dress in green; my lover also wears green). The miller responds to the miller maid's casual but significant comment – Müller has her speak in light, tripping poetic rhythms – by giving her the ribbon immediately as a kind of chivalric guerdon and finding in its colour all the symbolism of hope and eternity. Now the lad has another actual encounter, however inconsequential, with which to fortify his love and a momentary solution to his creative dilemma. What had formerly belonged to art (the lute) now belongs to her, the Samson-like act of cutting the ribbon and sending it to her additionally laden with sexual symbolism of self-surrender and emasculation. In tragic irony, the gift he sends her as symbolically representative of himself for her represents someone else. He has, he confides, not liked green before, but now, pathetically, he adopts it as *their* colour ('Drum haben *wir* es gern'). The alliterative r's and g's of 'Grün so gern' echo throughout the poem: some form of the phrase constitutes the third and sixth line of each six-line stanza, and those lines are in iambic trimeters rather than the tetrameters of lines 1–2, 4–5. Müller often underscores particularly significant words by shortening the poetic line at that point, an effect lost in musical setting.

14. Der Jäger (The hunter)

Was sucht denn der Jäger am Mühlbach hier?	What is the huntsman looking for here at the mill-stream?
Bleib', trotziger Jäger, in deinem Revier!	Stay, defiant hunter, in your own territory!
Hier gibt es kein Wild zu jagen für dich,	There is no game here for you to hunt;
Hier wohnt nur ein Rehlein, ein zahmes, für mich.	here lives only a little fawn, a tame one, for me.
Und willst du das zärtliche Rehlein sehn,	And if you wish to see the gentle fawn,

So laß deine Büchsen im Walde
 stehn,
Und laß deine klaffenden Hunde zu
 Haus,
Und laß auf dem Horne den Saus
 und Braus,
Und schere vom Kinne das struppige
 Haar,
Sonst scheut sich im Garten das
 Rehlein fürwahr.

Doch besser, du bliebest im Walde
 dazu,
Und ließest die Mühlen und Müller
 in Ruh'.
Was taugen die Fischlein im grünen
 Gezweig?
Was will denn das Eichhorn in
 bläulichen Teich?
Drum bleibe, du trotziger Jäger, im
 Hain,
Und laß mich mit meinen drei
 Rädern allein;
Und willst meinem Schätzchen dich
 machen beliebt,
So wisse, mein Freund, was ihr
 Herzchen betrübt:
Die Eber, die kommen zu Nacht aus
 dem Hain,
Und brechen in ihren Kohlgarten ein,
Und treten und wühlen herum in dem
 Feld:
Die Eber, die schieße, du Jägerheld!

then leave your guns in the forest,

and leave your baying hounds at
 home,
and stop that din and uproar on your
 horn
and shave the bristling hair from your
 chin,
or the fawn will surely hide in the
 garden.

But better you should stay in the
 forest,
and leave mills and millers in peace.

How can fishes thrive in green
 branches?
What can the squirrel want in the
 blue pond?
Then stay in the woods, you arrogant
 hunter,
and leave me alone with my three
 mill-wheels;
and if you would endear yourself to
 my sweetheart,
then know, my friend, what is
 troubling her heart:
wild boars come out of the woods by
 night
and break into her cabbage patch,
and trample and root about in the
 ground.
Those wild boars, shoot them, you
 heroic hunter!

The Other that Romantic passion always fears arrives in this poem. When the miller addresses the hunter in fancy (it is clear from the first line that the hunter is not actually present) as 'my friend', he is being sarcastic, but there is a deeper truth to the words. Passion in the medieval romances from which Müller derives the essence of his miller cycle does not lead to marriage, however much the lovers may ostensibly wish it, and therefore *requires* an insuperable obstacle between the lover and beloved. The hunter is thus a necessity, and he appears on cue.

John Reed speaks of 'jackboot rhythms' in Schubert's setting, and the phrase is apt as well for Müller's poetry, for the rapid, rattling lines in anapaestic tetrameters filled with percussive consonants (-t, -st, -d, -b, -tz) – the anapaests later impelled Schubert's choice of 6/8 metre to accommodate the wordy rush of anger.[1] The miller is so anxious that he begins straight away with a rhetorical question and the answer he already knows. In a telling choice of image, he characterizes the miller maid as a tame little fawn, that is, appropriate prey for hunters, and yet he still lays claim to her as *his* pet. Müller separates the adjective 'tame' from the noun it modifies in order to emphasize it ('ein Rehlein, *ein zahmes*, für mich'), the claim of possession all the more emphatic because threatened. The miller equates the hunter by implication with the wild beasts he hunts and instructs him that he will have to become civilized or else he will frighten his prey. Implicit in his miniature manual on etiquette is the outraged denial that the woman he loves might prefer such primitive, violent types to gentle beings like himself. In the contrast between the miller and the hunter is the deeper contrast between order and disorder, civilization and primeval urges that burst the bounds of society's wall.

Between stanzas 1 and 2, the miller realizes that he is actually advising the man he detests how best to court the miller's daughter, how to become acceptable in polite society, and instead tells the hunter to be gone. He is not in his element outside the forest and should not even want to remain. As if compelled, however, the miller repeats the pattern from the first stanza and once again instructs the hunter how to ingratiate himself with the miller maid by heroic deeds on her behalf, a disturbing revelation that the miller already counts the contest lost to him. He has earlier lamented his lack of physical heroism in 'Am Feierabend' and knows he cannot compete on that, or any other, level. Having defined his world as that of well-mannered civility, unlike the brutish primitivism of the hunter, the miller is only able to express his fury and desire for aggression at the level of symbolic displacement. The boars who come out from the forest at night and tear up the domestic, ordered tranquillity of civilized people are clearly equated with the hunter himself, as hairy and frightening as the most boorish beast. In the miller's injunction to shoot them, one hears his murderous wish that he could kill the *hunter* instead. That the miller's fury is sexual in origin is made clear in Müller's brilliant formal stroke of invention here at the close of the poem: the ten lines of stanza 1 overflow into an extra couplet in stanza 2 at the sexualized images of despoilment, 'treten und wühlen', the miller can no longer keep at bay.

As so often, Müller borrows an existing literary theme and devises his own variations on it. In German folksong and the Romantic poetry modelled on it, the hunter is the epitome of freedom, unregulated by society, a king unto himself in Nature's realm, beyond the reach of civilization's sexual, governmental, and religious constraints. But the miller does not celebrate the archetype: he castigates it. For him, the hunter exemplifies, not the perfect compound of Liberty and Nature, but the darkest instincts run rampant in the *selva oscura* beyond civilization's reach.

15. Eifersucht und Stolz (Jealousy and pride)

Wohin so schnell, so kraus, so wild
   [so kraus und wild], mein lieber
   Bach?
Eilst du voll Zorn dem frechen
   Bruder Jäger nach?
Kehr um, kehr um und schilt erst
   deine Müllerin
Für ihren leichten, losen, kleinen
   Flattersinn.
Sahst du sie gestern Abend nicht am
   Tore stehn,
Mit langem Halse nach der großen
   Straße sehn?
Wenn von dem Fang der Jäger lustig
   zieht nach Haus,
Da steckt kein sittsam Kind den Kopf
   zum Fenster 'naus.
Geh Bächlein hin und sag ihr das,
   doch sag ihr nicht,
Hörst du, kein Wort von meinem
   traurigen Gesicht;
Sag ihr: Er schnitzt bei mir sich eine
   Pfeif' aus Rohr
Und bläst den Kindern schöne Tänz
   und Lieder vor.
[Sag ihr's, sag ihr's, sag ihr's!]

Whither so fast, so ragged and wild,
   my dear stream?
Are you hurrying angrily after that
   shameless brother huntsman?
Turn round, turn round, and first
   scold your miller maid
for her frivolous, wanton fickleness!

Didn't you see her standing at the
   gate last night,
craning her neck as she looked down
   the high road?
When the hunter comes merrily home
   from the chase,
then no good girl puts her head out of
   the window.
Go there, brook, and tell her that, but
   don't tell her –
not a word, do you hear? – of my sad
   face.
Tell her: he is on my banks, carving a
   reed whistle
and playing lovely songs and dances
   for the children.
[Tell her that, tell her, tell her!]

Anger impels a rush of words. The lines in trimeters and tetrameters that one finds in the shy, ardent love poems are replaced by a tirade in hexameters, a single furious stanza without breathing room for stanzaic divisions. Every element of the language and form creates the impression of angry emphasis: the masculine endings clip each line closed, as in 'Der Jäger', and there is an unusually large number of single-syllable words throughout the poem, the miller painfully, angrily spitting out a floodtide of terse words through clenched teeth. The poetic control Müller exercises over the poetic rhythm is especially evident in such places as the misery-laden accumulation of adjectives to characterize the miller maid's fickle-ness: 'leichten, losen, kleinen Flattersinn', with its complex compound of fluent liquid -l's and hammered trochaic beats. The pained directive 'Kehr um, kehr um', with its emphatic -k's and the darkened vowel -u, is actually a plea to this representative of 'the river of Time' to turn back the clock to return to a time before the hunter's arrival when the miller could still delude himself that she was his.

The miller turns to his friend the brook for consolation and aid as a message-bearer, but he also relegates the hunter and the miller maid alike to the brook's realm of amoral Nature. The hunter is the brook's 'brother', and the maiden is '*your* miller maid' (deine Müllerin); in their wicked sensuality, they have renounced the mores proper to society and become natural beings unmindful of civilized behavior, a condemnable metamorphosis in the miller's eyes. The poem is furthermore a psycho-logically acute study of a distraught person's changes of mind, of the way competing claims of jealousy and pride push one now this way, now that. At the end, the miller speaks in pained self-mockery when he bids the stream to deploy reverse psychology and tell the fickle creature that the miller plays merry songs and dances for children. The 'beautiful songs and dances' are songs of the miller and lovely miller maid in happier times, songs he will sing in a self-consciously naive manner to 'children'. Only children, he implies, believe in faithful love, and he is no longer a child.

15a. Erster Schmerz, letzter Scherz (First Sorrow, Last Jest) – the second poem Schubert omitted from the body of the narrative

Writers on Schubert often cite its length and the fact that it introduces no new themes or plot developments as possible reasons for Schubert's decision to omit this poem from his cycle. 'Erster Schmerz, letzter Scherz' is one of the 'new songs' inspired by love's sorrow, foretold in 'Pause', and I wonder whether Schubert felt that there were perhaps too many 'new songs' en route to the dénouement in death.

16. Die liebe Farbe (The beloved colour)

In Grün will ich mich kleiden,	I will dress in green,
In grüne Tränenweiden,	in green weeping willows.
Mein Schatz hat's Grün so gern.	My love is so fond of green.
Will suchen einen Zypressenhain,	I'll seek out a cypress grove,
Eine Heide von grünem Rosmarein.	a heath filled with green rosemary.
Mein Schatz hat's Grün so gern.	My love is so fond of green.
Wohlauf zum fröhlichen Jagen	Up and away to the merry hunt!
Wohlauf durch Heid und Hagen!	Away over heath and hedge!
Mein Schatz hat's Jagen so gern.	My love is so fond of hunting.
Das Wild, das ich jage, das ist der Tod,	The game that I hunt is Death;
Die Heide, die heiß ich die Liebesnot.	the heath I call Love's Suffering.
Mein Schatz hat's jagen so gern.	My love is so fond of hunting.
Grabt mir ein Grab im Wasen,	Dig my grave in the grass,
Deckt mich mit grünem Rasen.	cover me with green turf.
Mein Schatz hat's Grün so gern.	My love is so fond of green.
Kein Kreuzlein schwarz, kein Blümlein bunt,	No black cross, no bright flowers,
Grün, alles grün so rings und rund [so ringsumher]!	green, everything green round about.
Mein Schatz hat's Grün so gern.	My love is so fond of green.

'Die liebe Farbe' is a variation of the medieval *Minnejagd* or *chasse d'amour* as a weary pursuit of Death – now the miller too can become a hunter. Intent both on obeying his sweetheart's every wish and punishing her for her perfidy, he contemplates a death that is the mirror image of Ophelia's, and the weeping willows, cypress, and rosemary that ring her watery grave grow again in his imagination. Because his beloved loves green and hunting, he shall die shrouded in green at the end of the hunt; masochism colours his despair in the hue of her choice. The traditional symbolic meanings are alchemically transformed in the last chapters of the tale: green is no longer the colours of hope, springtime, renewal, and love but the colour of death, the grassy mantle for his grave.

The six-line stanza and refrain structure of 'Mit dem grünen Lautenbande' recur here, impelled by the thought that she loves green (and those who wear it). But, unlike its antecedent, this poem is funereal in its rhythms as well as its imagery, screams of pain that have stuck in the throat, frozen grief. Müller imposes a pause at the end of each line, and the cumulative weight of the pauses drags down the poem in a distinctive fashion, unlike any other poem in the cycle – a death-knell even before Schubert's pedal point and ostinati. In each stanza, the mournful reiterations of the refrain, 'Mein Schatz hat's Grün so gern', itself weighed down by the alliterative -ts/-tz and -gr compound consonants, follow one couplet in iambic trimeters that ends with unaccented syllables and a second couplet in iambic and anapaestic tetrameters that ends, like the refrain, with accented syllables – what Cottrell calls 'patterned irregularities' in the formal structure, including the quickened anapaestic rhythms in the second stanza, preclude monotony (Cottrell, 24). Schubert does not, one notices, acknowledge the rhythmic energy of these cries to rouse the hunt, but rather subsumes all differences of poetic tone in the same funeral pall throughout the entire song.

17. Die böse Farbe (The evil colour)

Ich möchte ziehn in die Welt hinaus,
Hinaus in die weite Welt!
Wenn's nur so grün, so grün nicht wär,
Da draußen in Wald und Feld.

I'd like to go out into the world,
into the wide world,
if only it were not so green, so green
out there in forest and field.

Ich möchte die grünen Blätter all

Pflücken von jedem Zweig,
Ich möchte die grünen Gräser all

Weinen ganz totenbleich.

I would like to pluck all the green
leaves
from every branch,
and I would like to make the green
grass
deathly pale with my weeping.

Ach Grün, du böse Farbe du,
Was siehst mich immer an,
So stolz, so keck, so schadenfroh,
Mich armen weißen Mann?

Ah green, you hateful colour,
why do you always look at me,
so proud, so bold, so gloating,
and me a poor white miller?

Ich möchte liegen vor ihrer Tür
In Sturm und Regen und Schnee,
Und singen ganz leise bei Tag und
Nacht
Das eine Wörtchen Ade.

I'd like to lie in front of her door
in the storm and rain and snow,
and day and night softly sing

one little word: Farewell.

Horch, wenn im Wald ein Jagdhorn
ruft [schallt],
Da klingt ihr Fensterlein,
Und schaut sie auch nach mir nicht
aus,

Hark, when a hunting horn resounds
in the forest,
there's the sound of her window then;
and though she doesn't look out to
see me,

Darf ich doch schauen hinein.	I can still look in.

O binde von der Stirn dir ab	O untie from your brow
Das grüne, grüne Band.	the green, green ribbon.
Ade, ade und reiche mir	Farewell, farewell, and give me
Zum Abschied deine Hand.	your hand in parting!

This last flare-up of desperate energy before the end is the consequence and antithesis of 'Die liebe Farbe'. The miller momentarily longs for flight from his sorrow and escape out into the unbounded world, away from the mill, but he is defeated by the omnipresent green of Nature. Everywhere he looks, he sees a world that belongs to the hunter, a world that has nothing to do with him. In despair, he sings of fantasy transformations – the phrase 'Ich möchte ... ich möchte' echoes throughout – by which he would forcibly make the landscape *his* reflection, *his* mirror, as barren of life as the skeletal branches, as floury-white as he himself. Continuing the alchemical colour transformations from the preceding poem, he would now displace the hope, life, and love that green represented with the white of winter and death: 'totenbleich'. As the culmination of his frantic desire to obliterate green from the world, he would have the miller maid remove the green ribbon he had earlier envisaged in her hair, the imperative 'O binde' both an order and a plea. The fantasized gesture is symbolic of his wish that the miller maid herself give up the hunter (again, the miller is passive, even in his own fantasies) – a wish that Schubert rightly interprets as bordering on madness. When the miller speaks to 'Green' as to an anthropomorphized presence that looks at him always, everywhere, one understands that Green is the hunter, whom the miller cannot bear to invoke directly. The imagined sound of the hunting horn and the green he sees/that sees him are enough to drive the miller to the brink of insanity.

Images of sight are everywhere in this poem. The miller, unable to see himself reflected in the miller maid's eyes, looks about frantically for evidence of his very existence and cannot find it. He cannot banish the thought of her 'looking' at the hunter, sight here a sexualized act; unable to relinquish the sight of her, he conjures up a tormenting image of himself as onlooker, unseen, unnoticed, unregarded. The voyeuristic vision in 'Erster Schmerz, letzter Scherz' of the miller as spectator in an erotic theatre *à deux* recurs but as an image akin to Edvard Munch's painting *Jealousy*, with its lovers who gaze at one another on the shore by a dark forest while the banished jealous one broods on the periphery. He too cannot stop staring at an inner vision that horrifies him.

'One little word' in 'Der Neugierige' was 'Yes' or 'No', either/or; now it too is transformed into 'Ade', a single word that excludes all other possibilities. In a fantasy of utter abnegation, a fantasy nineteenth-century readers would have construed as feminine in nature, he imagines lying in front of her door in the rain and storm and snow – it is the winter of the spirit for him now – singing the one word over and over again, in masochistic self-flagellating excess. The excess is also accusatory by implication: she would surely pay no heed to his farewell unless he repeated it many times, a verbal and musical assault on the wall of her indifference. The little word *Ade*, its diminutive size in ironic contrast with the enormity of what it signifies, is simultaneously a farewell to her and a farewell to life.

17a. Blümlein Vergissmein (Little forget-me flower) – the third poem Schubert omitted from the cycle

This poem is a vision of the mind's Hell before Death that Villiers de L'Isle-Adam would have been proud to claim – the poem is astonishingly premonitory of later Symbolist, even Surrealist, works. Müller carefully chooses his words to convey paranoia and painfully heightened erotic sensibility, voyeurism turned in upon itself and become pure suffering. The atmosphere is demonic, unlike anything else in the cycle, and Schubert may well have omitted it for that reason, as well as for its length.

18. Trock'ne Blumen (Withered flowers)

Ihr Blümlein alle,	You flowers all
Die sie mir gab,	that she gave to me,
Euch soll man legen	they must lay you
Mit mir ins Grab.	in the grave with me.
Wie seht ihr alle	Why do you look at me
Mich an so weh,	so sadly,
Als ob ihr wüßtet,	as if you knew
Wie mir gescheh'?	what had happened to me?
Ihr Blümlein alle,	All you flowers,
Wie welk, wie blaß?	why withered, why pale?
Ihr Blümlein alle,	All you flowers,
Wovon so naß?	wherefore so wet?
Ach, Tränen machen	Alas, tears do not create
Nicht maiengrün,	Maytime green,
Machen tote Liebe	do not make dead love
Nicht wieder blühn.	bloom again.

Und Lenz wird kommen,	And spring will come,
Und Winter wird gehn,	and winter will pass,
Und Blümlein werden	and flowers will grow
Im Grase stehn.	in the grass.
Und Blümlein liegen	And flowers will lie
In meinem Grab,	on my grave,
Die Blümlein alle,	all the flowers
Die sie mir gab. [!]	that she gave me.
Und wenn sie wandelt	And when she walks
Am Hügel vorbei	past the mound
Und denkt im Herzen,	and ponders in her heart:
Der meint' es treu!	'His love was true!'
Dann Blümlein alle,	Then all you flowers,
Heraus, heraus,	come out, come out!
Der Mai ist kommen,	May has come
Der Winter ist aus.	and winter is past.

This poem, which belongs to the earliest layer of the cycle, is the miller's attempt to exorcise the demons of 'Blümlein Vergissmein' and to find a meaning for good in his impending death. The resurrection he imagines here is expressed with an economy unlike his youthful fervour or the outpourings of jealous anger. Read aloud, the quatrains in dimeter lines become rhyming couplets in tetrameters; Müller evidently wanted the stark effect of the shorter lines, the austerity of all that extra white space on the page. The love for which the miller lays down his life will, he asserts, eventually be reciprocated after all, will flower and bloom in the maiden's heart after his death. Only when she sees the flowers on his grave will she realize and respond to his love. This is Romantic love, unattainable in life.

But does he believe it? Once again, Müller's poetic language merits a closer look. When the miller speaks to the flowers 'that she gave me', one can understand the statement both as fact and as the continued identification of the miller maid with the metonymic flower-eyes that 'wink and blink' from the river bank. This is yet another poem about seeing and knowing, sight and recognition. In his vision of resurrection, the miller imagines that the flowers symbolic of his love will bloom anew from his grave-mound; when she sees them, she will at last understand their symbolic import. But the miller cannot imagine the miller maid saying to herself, 'He loved me', but rather the untranslatable 'der meint' es treu'. The antecedent of 'es' is love, but he dare not say the word directly. Nor, as we discover in the next poem, is he able to sustain belief in the epiphany he envisages here.

19. Der Müller und der Bach (The miller and the brook)

Der Müller:
Wo ein treues Herze
In Liebe vergeht,
Da welken die Lilien
Auf jedem Beet;

Da muß in die Wolken
Der Vollmond gehn,
Damit seine Tränen
Die Menschen nicht sehn;

Da halten die Englein
Die Augen sich zu
Und schluchzen und singen
Die Seele zu Ruh'.

Der Bach:
Und wenn sich die Liebe
Dem Schmerz entringt,
Ein Sternlein, ein neues,
Am Himmel erblinkt;

Da springen drei Rosen,
Halb rot, [und] halb weiß,
Die welken nicht wieder
Aus Dornenreis.

Und die Engelein schneiden
Die Flügel sich ab
Und gehn alle Morgen
Zur Erde herab.

Der Müller:
Ach, Bächlein, liebes Bächlein,
Du meinst es so gut:
Ach, Bächlein, aber weißt du,
Wie Liebe tut?

Ach unten, da unten
Die kühle Ruh'!
Ach, Bächlein, liebes Bächlein,
So singe nur zu.

The miller:
When a true heart
dies of love,
then lilies wither
in their beds;

The full moon
must vanish behind the clouds
so that people
do not see its tears;

There, angels
shut their eyes
and sob and sing
the soul to rest.

The brook:
And when love
wrests free of sorrow,
a new star
shines in the sky;

Three roses,
half red and half white, spring
from thorny stems
and never wither.

And the angels
cut off their wings
and descend to earth
every morning.

The miller:
Ah brook, beloved brook,
you mean so well,
but do you know, brook,
what love can do?

Ah, below, down below,
is cool rest!
Oh brook, beloved brook,
sing on!

This is an inner debate of life versus death in which the brook, the voice of Nature, argues for continued life and the miller for death. One can understand both voices, however, as emanating from within the miller himself, the internal *agon* of someone on the verge of suicide. Significantly, he speaks for death and assigns the voice of life to an external agency, to eternal Nature. As in 'Trock'ne Blumen', whose short-breathed poetic metres he repeats here, he looks for meaning in death and imagines both heaven and earth reacting either to his death or his triumph over pain. Because he searches for ultimate significance, he speaks in symbols: the stars of love that are either hidden in clouds or newly apparent, the withered or eternally blossoming flowers, the angels who weep in heaven or live on earth and move among us in human form. In particular, the countervailing argument for life impels an especially intense cluster of symbols, including the mystic number three, the roses of love, a thorny sprig emblematic of the inevitable pain of love and life, and the paired colours red and white – the red of pain, blood, and passion and the lily white of innocence and purity. But once again, as in 'Am Feierabend' and 'Mein!', the assertion of vitality collapses with the quadruple exclamations 'Ach' in the last two stanzas. The miller can no longer sustain belief in the ecstatic vision of future apotheosis he has proposed in 'Trock'ne Blumen'. At the end of the poem, the youth imagines death as a letting-go, as the dissolution of life into a flood of music ('So singe nur zu'). The lulling sound of the -u's, the -z sounds of 'So singe', the gently rocking repetitions ('unten, da unten', 'Bächlein, liebes Bächlein') anticipate the word-music of the final poem. In the earliest published version of 'Der Müller und der Bach', the heartbroken miller in the last stanza invokes 'die *heimische* Ruh' (home-like peace) down below; Müller later changed the adjective to 'kühle' in the final version, evocative of chill Death and water as the cooling agent for Life's fever. The theme of Death as home-coming is thus reserved for the lullaby that follows.

20. Des Baches Wiegenlied (The brook's lullaby)

Gute Ruh', gute Ruh'!	Rest well, rest well,
Tu die Augen zu!	close your eyes!
Wandrer, du müder, du bist zu Haus.	Wanderer, weary one, you are home.
Die Treu ist hier,	Here is fidelity;
Sollst liegen bei mir,	you shall lie with me
Bis das Meer will trinken die Bächlein aus.	until the sea drinks up all the brooks.

Will betten dich kühl
Auf weichem [weichen] Pfühl,
In dem blauen kristallenen Kämmerlein.
Heran, heran,
Was wiegen kann,
Woget und wieget den Knaben mir ein!

I will make you a cool bed
on a soft pillow
in the blue, crystalline chamber.
Come here, come,
all who can lull
and rock this boy for me!

Wenn ein Jagdhorn schallt
Aus dem grünen Wald,
Will ich sausen und brausen wohl um
    dich her.
Blickt nicht herein (hinein),
Blaue Blümelein!
Ihr macht meinem Schläfer die
    Träume so schwer.

When a hunting horn sounds
from the green forest,
I will gush and roar all around you.

Do not look within,
little blue flowers!
You will make my sleeper's dreams so
    troubled.

Hinweg, hinweg
Von dem Mühlensteg,
Böses Mägdlein [Mägdelein], daß ihn
    dein Schatten nicht weckt!
Wirf mir herein
Dein Tüchlein fein,
Daß ich die Augen ihm halte bedeckt!

Away, away
from the mill path,
wicked girl, lest your shadow wake
    him!
Throw me
your fine shawl
that I may keep his eyes covered.

Gute Nacht, gute Nacht!
Bis alles wacht.
Schlaf aus deine Freude, schlaf aus
    dein Leid!
Der Vollmond steigt,
Der Nebel weicht,
Und der Himmel da droben [oben],
    wie ist er so weit!

Good night, good night!
Until all awaken.
Sleep away your joy, sleep away your
    sorrow!
The full moon is rising,
the mist vanishes,
and the sky above, how vast it is!

Müller had a knack for ending cycles with his finest efforts. Once again, he writes a poem of death and rebirth, but one different in imagery and tone from 'Trock'ne Blumen'. A majestic spiritual vision unfolds calmly, unforgettably, at the close of the tale.

Schubert's setting obliterates the distinctive six-line stanza of 'Des Baches Wiegenlied':

a
a these two rhyming dimeter lines vary rhythmically from verse to verse

b single line of tetrameters, again in varying rhythms

c
c another pair of rhyming lines in dimeters

b a closing line of tetrameters that rhymes with line 3

The metrical variations are considerable. For example, the first line consists of a repeated anapaest, its lulling -u sounds the ingress to a mournful but peaceful atmosphere. The third line, however, begins with a single trochee ('*Wand*'rer'), its accented initial syllable answered by the corresponding stress at the end of the line on the word 'Haus' – for Müller's wanderers, the ultimate symbol of blessedness. The third line of the accusatory fourth stanza reverts, in deliberate reminiscence, to the angry hexameters of 'Eifersucht und Stolz', when he bids the brook scold the wicked maiden. Here, the brook bans the miller maid, the cause of all this grief, from the scene (but she was almost never present!). The singular longer line creates a problem for composers in literal strophic forms, a problem Schubert solves brilliantly. When he repeats the paired dimeter lines 'Hinweg, hinweg / Von dem Mühlensteg', he puts the words 'Böses Mägdelein' in place of the prepositional phrase 'von dem Mühlensteg'. For musical purposes, the middle line is this: 'Daß ihn dein Schatten, *dein Schatten* nicht weckt'. The extra emphasis of Schubert's repetition is wonderfully expressive of love and lingering obsession all in one.

In 'Der Müller und der Bach', the miller at the end bids the brook 'sing on', that is, continue singing to him after his death. 'Des Baches Wiegenlied' enacts the moment of death so that we see, as one with the dying youth, a vision of ultimate unity in a realm beyond time and space. Life's voyage is over, its goal the sea of eternity ('Bis das Meer will trinken die Bächlein aus'). Mother Nature will welcome him, shelter and protect him, assure him ultimate surcease because she is eternal as well as temporal and can thus speak of the world beyond death. This is Wordsworth's 'the speaking face of earth and heaven', the Book of Nature which promises a secret sense and a resurrection which returns us to unity with ourselves and with the natural world. The death-green is banished, and the blue of the beloved's eyes, the flowers, and the heavens envelops the youth in a crystal casket, the alliterative hard -k's of 'kristallenen Kämmerlein' evocative of a quality distinct from the watery element of the brook. There, he will be rocked as in a cradle by the water spirits the youth first heard in stanza 5 of 'Wohin?', summoned by gentle waves of repetition. In the crystal cradle, all emotion – the polarities of 'Freud' and 'Leid', a commonplace in Müller's verse, encompass the entire gamut of feeling – will be dispelled for eternity.

The majestic moonrise at the end tells of the final interweaving of the cosmos and human souls in the afterlife, a vision prefigured in 'Tränenregen' when the poet weaves together the moon, stars, flowers, and the beloved's eyes within the brook, the flowing symbol of eternity. Now we understand the title: this is a lullaby to a new-born and higher life. The mist, symbolic of all that evades understanding in life, gives way before the monumentally-conceived rising of the moon, its mysterious powers vanquishing the mist and revealing infinity. Cottrell points out that the poem and thus the body of the cycle end with the adjective 'weit', with the expansion into the infinite. The assonance of the end-words 'Leid', 'steigt', 'weicht', and 'weit' in the final stanza, a musical confluence of tones that bespeaks the dissolution of boundaries, hinges upon the diphthong '-ei', a succession of two vowels in motion, dissolved into one sound that escapes the static state of isolation and rises into the air as pure tone (Cottrell, 30–1).

20a. Der Dichter, als Epilog (The poet, as epilogue)

Like the Prosperos and Pucks who ring down the curtain at the close of the play, the Poet returns for the Epilogue, feigning Pirandello-like disgruntlement that the brook has usurped his role – poets should pronounce whatever funeral oration is required, not characters – and dampened everyone's spirits in the process. All that's left for him is to bring the playgoers back to reality by reminding them for the last time that all they have heard is make-believe, the stuff of dreams. Adept at authorial twists and turns, he nonetheless sneaks a concluding moral in through the back door and ends the work by hoping (in company with all writers) that his Everyman saga has left its imprint on the audience, specifically, men, who should learn from it to be all the more grateful for the gift of requited love. For women, this is, however obliquely implied, a post-Romantic permutation of the traditional cautionary fables about the consequences of love denied, fables that assume women's generic sinful sensuality and heartlessness. Even as the poet seems to relent at the close and to speak kindly of the dead, he nonetheless counsels his readers to prefer the substance over the shadow and real love in life to death-dealing Romantic passion in verse. He has, he hints, created an illusion that his readers might appreciate the goodness of love in actual experience all the more, might step back from the brink over which his poor miller has fallen.

In a final literary twist, Müller versifies any and all poets' ambivalence towards their own creations, orders in rhyme and rhythms the poet's love-hate compound of dissatisfaction coupled with hopes for immortality. May the miller – and, of course, the poet as well – live forever in generation after generation of readers' hearts, there defying death, he proclaims openly at the end. It is both cleverly done and touching, but Schubert preferred to eliminate the literary middleman when he discovered Müller's verse and found it 'komponabel'. Music and the poetic tale itself could make their own case for immortality.

5

The music of 'Die schöne Müllerin'

The term 'song cycle' is a notoriously malleable designation: it signifies a group of songs that belong together but in ways that defy easy definitions of genre. Some are poetic narratives, some not; some are settings of poems by a single poet, while others are compilations from different poetic sources.[1] Many are not cyclic at all in the sense that music from earlier in the work returns at a later point, and the musical relationships between songs, where they exist, vary widely as well. Both of Schubert's Müller cycles, *sui generis* in their architecture, consist of a lengthy sequence of independent songs, as challenging in both length and musical complexity as any work in the larger, more established classical genres. Each song presents one moment of intense emotion, one stage in the story, paradoxically complete but *more* complete in context. 'In the life of the mind, no one moment is exactly like any other', Richard Capell observed of *Winterreise*, and the same is true of the first Müller-cycle.[2]

There are, however, other sources of unity, neither stringently observed nor all-embracing but present nevertheless. Tonal unity is always a vexed question, but there seems little doubt that certain tonalities have dramatic significance within the cycle. Schubert's willingness to transpose songs for Vogl, Schönstein, and others should not be confused with an uncaring attitude regarding the choice of tonality for the songs of *Die schöne Müllerin*, as exigencies gladly tolerated for the sake of performance do not therefore negate the composer's ideal designs. The cycle is, appropriately, a linear march forward, not a closed circle: the E major of death and resurrection at the end only appears for the first time as a principal tonality in the last half of 'Trock'ne Blumen', and it is as far as possible from the Bb major of 'Das Wandern', a tonal symbol of the distance between life and death.[3] Within that span, Schubert links occasional pairs or trios of songs (not the entire cycle) by tonality, beginning with nos. 9 and 10, 'Des Müllers Blumen' and 'Tränenregen': both are in A major, intermingled with parallel minor at the end of the latter song. A major, 'the key which unlocked the essential

Schubert', has already appeared in 'Ungeduld' and is associated in this cycle with love and Nature co-mingled, the maiden's blue eyes and the brook's flowers fused together.[4] The Bb major tonality that links nos. 12 and 13, 'Pause' and 'Mit dem grünen Lautenbande', with the repeated image of the lute and its green strap, is foreshadowed by the abrupt shift to Bb major in the B section of 'Mein!'. ('Mein!' is one of Schubert's few songs in D major and is the only occurrence of the key as a principal tonality in the entire cycle.) Nos. 16 and 17, 'Die liebe Farbe' and 'Die böse Farbe', are set in parallel major and minor modes of B – the same tonic, but antithetical moods.

Tonalities are also used to separate songs, to heighten changes of place, tone, time, and temper by means of tonal disjunction. When the right-hand part of 'Wohin?' begins on the B a semitone above the Bbs with which 'Das Wandern' ended, we hear the shift as indicative of another place, removed from that of the first song. The B major of 'Der Neugierige' follows the A minor of 'Am Feierabend'; the tonal contrast underscores the difference between the feverish impatience of one and the pensive mood of the other. The miller's C minor imprecations against the hunter in no. 15, 'Der Jäger', succeed the graceful insipidity of 'Mit dem grünen Lautenbande' in Bb major and shatter its aftermath. If the C major of 'Halt!' and 'Morgengruß' is associated with sunlit clarity and hopefulness, then C minor is its antithesis.

Some commentators have pointed to the fact that *Die schöne Müllerin* is framed on either side by strophic songs and includes six others (nos. 7, 8, 9, 13, 15, 16 – no. 10 also is strict strophic with a final varied stanza) as evidence of the miller's naiveté and innocence.[5] The miller is not, however, a rustic simpleton, and the subtleties of Schubert's musical strophes, as in 'Ungeduld' and 'Morgengruß', attest to his recognition of a complex emotional life in Müller's verses. In those two songs and others ('Das Wandern', for example, or Schubert's setting of the first six poetic stanzas/ three musical strophes of 'Tränenregen'), the youth elaborates a single idea, feeling, or thought throughout the poem; hence, Schubert uses strophic form, but always with psychologically rich nuances incompatible with true *Volkstümlichkeit*. Elsewhere in the cycle, varied strophic form and three-part song form prevail; it is interesting to see that other composers did not set poems for which strophic form would not have been suitable, such as 'Am Feierabend', 'Mein!', 'Pause', and 'Eifersucht und Stolz' (see the bibliography for a select list of other settings of poems from *Die schöne Müllerin*).

1. Das Wandern – Mäßig geschwind, 2/4, Bb major

This is pre-lapsarian *Wanderlust* in music, although there are more compositional subtleties than its inclusion in books of German student songs (*Commersbücher*) and folksong anthologies might suggest. The figuration in the introduction, with its 'striding' broken octaves in the bass and ceaseless motion, divides into a topmost melodic line and broken chordal accompaniment, in other words, not purely accompanimental figures; the jaunty offbeat placement of the melody pitches, especially the 'double stops' (the thirds and sixths) in the right hand, belies the seeming folk-like squareness of phrase construction.[6] Schubert suggests the youth's energy and freshness of purpose in the athleticism of the first vocal phrase (bars 5–7, repeated in bars 9–11), rather ungrateful to sing on its own because it is so intertwined with the piano part as a single construct. In the introduction/interludes/postlude, Schubert repeats a two-bar unit that begins with the tonic harmony on the downbeat of the first bar and ends on the second beat of the second bar, also with the tonic harmony. The downbeat that follows makes the mid-bar ending of each two-bar unit sound like a separate miniature bar in 1/4, and yet both the beginning and end of the repeated pattern are tonic harmonies in close succession. The result is a rhythmic motor hypothetically capable of continuation without end, a perfect musical symbol for *Wanderlust*. The journey has not begun, however, and each stanza therefore begins with the musical version of 'walking-in-place', motion that is nonetheless rooted to the spot. Not until the words 'Das muß ein schlechter Müller sein' does a chord other than tonic or dominant appear, but there is no modulation, no change of tonal place.

Müller heightens the key words of each verse by an abruptly shortened refrain line, but Schubert has other means of emphasis. The refrain is always an authentic cadence, the assertions of tonal strength a stamp to seal each declarative statement ('To wander is the miller's joy – *to wander*'). At the end of each stanza, Schubert repeats the refrains fourfold, complete with a pianissimo echo, and there lengthens the accented syllable to a crotchet, emphasizing words with a near-magical power for the miller – stones, wheels, water, wandering – in yet another way. The fourfold repetition is incantatory: Schubert's miller casts a spell on himself by repeating key-words of great suggestivity and then ventures forth under their sway.

2. **Wohin?** – Mäßig, 2/4, G major

Schubert retains the 2/4 metre and the quaver–semiquaver motion that connote wandering in the first song, but with variations such as the open fifths in the bass rather than octaves, overlapping crotchets in the bass rather than quavers, and triplet semiquavers. The reflective question 'Where to?' banishes the self-propulsive forward drive of 'Das Wandern' and replaces it with rustling (*rauschendes*) motion in broken triadic patterns, a cliché of Nature music but one that Schubert revitalizes with the following refinements:

1. The rising-and-falling pattern of the brook's babbling continues seamlessly throughout the intricate formal structure of this song, with its complex recurrence of previous figures. Not until the poet moves from observation of the brook to wonderment in bars 11ff ('Ich weiß nicht, wie mir wurde') does the piano figuration move away from the hypnotically reiterated G major harmony of bars 1–10 – yet another musical spell – to such harmonic indices of uncertainty, of mysterious possibility, as the diminished seventh chord in bar 12 ('wurde').

2. The open fifths in the bass are broken into a rocking figure in which the upper pitch is sustained across the barline whenever the tonic harmony recurs as a bass ostinato for several bars or more – a lure to follow onwards even when the harmonies are static.

3. The sound of the dominant harmony over a tonic bass has already appeared in 'Das Wandern' and does so again much later in the cycle when the miller and the brook are together once again, but in a tragically altered atmosphere. In bars 1–7 of no. 19, 'Der Müller und der Bach', the same harmonies recur but in the minor and frozen in place, without the flowing motion of 'Wohin?'.

4. The youth's folk-like declamation on repeated notes and sturdily triadic contours in stanzas 1 and 2 harmonize with but are distinct from the brook's rustling.

As long as the focus is on the brook, the music remains diatonic, but with the first mention of the youth himself, the diatonicism is destabilized by the first chromaticism of the song. The ready availability of different harmonic avenues via diminished seventh chords is especially apropos here, as the youth does not know where the brook will take him. Here in bars 12ff, there is no modulation, no new tonality, but the heightening of supertonic A minor harmonies is a notable touch of minor; one notices as well the descending diminished fourth traced in the vocal line for bars 11–12. The indices of grief to come are subtle, but present nevertheless. In bar 15, furthermore, the measured trill on the upper neighbour note in the vocal line at the word 'mußte' (I *had* to go down there too) underscores the sense of compulsion.

At the beginning of stanza 3 in bars 23–5 ('Hinunter und immer weiter / und immer dem Bache nach'), the vocal line doubles the bass an octave higher. As if compelled, the youth mirrors, not the brook's surface babbling, but the depths beneath where he will eventually end his life. 'Hinunter' is the realm of death, and the E minor harmonies of bars 23–4 (supertonic of V, the tonality of the B section) are the first distant presage of the E minor tonality of 'Trock'ne Blumen'. The same phrase is repeated in the fourth stanza when the youth addresses the brook directly, saying 'With your babbling you have quite bemused my mind' – compulsion yet again, all the stronger because this time, there is a modulation to E minor, yet another premonition. Even though one only locates the relationship across the wide span between opposite ends of the cycle in retrospect, it can seem meaningful to those receptive to such long-range resemblances.

The same phrase returns for the last time in bars 62ff at the words 'Laß singen, Gesell, laß rauschen', the poet's ambivalence preserved in music: either the brook or the youth himself says to disregard the siren-song and walk on, but the lingering pull of compulsion still underlies the words. Not until he reminds himself of the 'mill-wheels in every clear stream' does the youth separate himself from the voices in the depths and resume his own musical identity. Wonderfully, he enacts 'wandering happily after' ('fröhlich nach') by echoing the cadential tag end; in particular, the final sustained dominant pitch in the vocal line, poised above the continued rustling of the brook, is a concise, lovely evocation of *Wanderlust*.

3. Halt! – Nicht zu geschwind, 6/8, C major

The miller finds the mill he was seeking, but is unsure whether to stay. The brook has led him to this place, and its incessant semiquaver motion continues, not only throughout this song but the next as well. As in 'Wohin?', the miller first hears or sees something Schubert makes audible in the lengthy piano introduction (sight for the poet becomes sound for the composer), with its two contrasting figures. The *forte* figure, onomatopoeia for the turning of the mill-wheel, derives its character from the emphatic downbeat and from the upper neighbour-note to the topmost note of the chord in each turn of the wheel. (Eight years earlier, Schubert had energized the intial figuration for the piano in 'Erlkönig' by similar means.) The accented upbeats in the bass for the contrasting soft figures are another index of psychic turmoil, for all the emphasis on each pulsation of the 6/8 metre – there are rhythmic markers of unrest aplenty. Momentary touches of G minor darken the atmosphere, briefly and *pianissimo*, both in 'Halt!' (bars 5–6) and 'Danksagung an den Bach'; later in the cycle, the contrast of G major and G minor is developed at greater length. One notices that the miller greets the 'sweet mill song' in bars 23–30 (Schubert's miller repeats his enthusiastic greeting more often than the poet) to dominant harmonies, the key of the 'Danksagung' to follow; there as well, the vocal line and accompaniment join in symbolic accord, the youth already binding himself to the mill. This passage ends on V of V (a D major chord) in bar 30, and that secondary dominant harmony is then followed by the natural form of the supertonic in C major (D minor). The darkening effect of the minor invests the words 'Und das Haus wie so traulich, / und die Fenster wie blank' with an added intensity of feeling, and the yearning appoggiatura of '*trau* - lich' adds yet another touch of intensification. When the focus moves from the slight but significant hint of tragedy awaiting within the house, four bars (bars 31–6) of D minor, to the bright external world ('und die Sonne, wie helle vom Himmel sie scheint'), the vocal line assumes a leaping, buoyant character, even more pronounced than the initial phrase of 'Das Wandern', and the music returns to C major. The youth still feels the attraction of wandering out in the open, and Schubert makes the attraction evident in this unshadowed *plein-air* passage.

In the final section of this through-composed song (bars 46–60), the miller asks over and over, 'Ei Bächlein, liebes Bächlein, war es also gemeint?'; since music tolerates, indeed demands, more repetition than poetry, Schubert's miller, frustrated by the lack of an answer, can and does repeat the question. Schubert each time places the accented syllable of '*al* - so' on the first beat and prolongs it, as if to say 'Is this *really*, *truly* what you meant?', and the Ab ($b6$) in the diminished seventh chord over the tonic bass expressively darkens the question in harmonic colorations of doubt. And yet, he also asks the question as if it were a certainty, a repeated cadence with tonic closure in the vocal line.

4. Danksagung an den Bach – Etwas langsam, 2/4, G major

The miller's doubts resolved, Schubert brings back the tonality, the motion in the piano that flows without a pause until the end, the 2/4 metre, and the open fifths and broken octaves in the bass of the second song. The antecedent of 'es' in the recurring question 'War es also gemeint?', however, has changed; where it formerly meant 'to stay at this mill', it now means 'to meet the miller maid'. Schubert consequently re-casts the D–C–B–C pitches of the vocal cadence at the end of 'Halt!' and has the piano and vocal part walk hand in hand (or perhaps flow) together. Three times in five bars (bars 5–10), the miller asks 'War es also gemeint?', but without the sense of wonder and disturbance from before, without the demand that destiny yield its secrets. Even though the vocal line ascends to high G, the repetition of the question brings it back down to the middle register and tonic closure, devoid of any true questioning inflection; both the rapturous ascent and the subsequent descent culminate in tonic closure, hardly indicative of uncertainty. The mill-wheel figure, the broken triad-plus-upper neighbour, reappears in rhythmic augmentation and in the vocal line at the words 'rauschender Freund' in bar 6 and again in bar 34 at the words 'hab' ich genug'. Here, it has calmed down and lacks the downbeat energies and driving compulsion of the figure in 'Halt!'. The contentment of stanza 5 – 'I have all I need for my hands and my heart alike' – is set to a repetition of the music for stanza 1; the grateful dismissal, for the moment, of all nagging questions of Fate and its mysterious operations is already implicit in the question he asks at the start.

And yet, the doubts linger throughout stanzas 2 and 3 and with them, other words and varied tones for the universal query, 'Is this what I am meant to do with my life?' Schubert ingeniously combines a three-part ABA song form with strophic variations, the final A section a significantly abbreviated return to the beginning. The refusal to ask any more questions cuts short the three-part form while the music of stanza 1 frames the texted body on either side in a balanced structure. Between those twin poles of diatonic surety, Schubert interposes tonal motion and strophic variation as the miller first asks whether the brook and the miller maid are collaborators, equally instruments of his fate, then reassures himself and returns to G major. The miller never leaves G major long enough to establish another tonality, but one nevertheless hears the sequences and secondary dominants in stanza 2 as questing-questioning movement and the brief incursions of parallel minor and Bb major in stanza 3 both as emblems of a slightly darkened seriousness and a reference to the tonality of 'Das Wandern'. Was it for this that the brook bade him wander four songs ago? In stanza 2 (bars 11–18), the perfect fourths and fifths from stanza 1 are bent into tritones (bars 11–12), the sequence in those bars a clever means both to distinguish and to link together the statements 'zur Müllerin hin, / so lautet der Sinn'. Arnold Feil has already discussed the startling effect of the exclamation 'Gelt', extended throughout bar 13, while the piano anticipates bar 14: the disruption of the phrase-structure as well as the prolongation of the single syllable for an entire bar makes apparent the desire for an answer in the affirmative. The downbeat stress on the word 'Hab' [ich's verstanden]' each time in bars 14–15 – *Have* I understood it? – is yet another form of questioning emphasis but one that leads to the G major cadence of bars 8–10. The 'es' of 'War es also gemeint?' is thus clarified as 'Zur Müllerin hin'.

The miller thinks in polarities: either the miller maid has sent the brook to fetch him or the brook has enchanted him, an enchantment he has already sensed in 'Wohin?'. Awareness of the brook's powers to enchant impels the brief turn to parallel minor, but the choice the miller prefers is evident when Schubert takes the lowered third degree B♭ and turns it into the brighter relative major in order to repeat 'ob sie dich geschickt, ob sie dich geschickt'. Here the word 'sie' (she) is the apex of the cadential phrase; in stanza 4, as the miller dismisses altogether the impulse to question, the F♮ is reinterpreted harmonically en route to G major on the verb 'surrender': 'ich *ge* - be mich drein'. What he wants to surrender to is the miller maid; the close proximity of the phrases and the evocative sound of the lowered leading-note subtly underline the link between them.

5. Am Feierabend – Ziemlich geschwind, 6/8, A minor

This is the first song in which the miller's emotions change radically in the course of the song; consequently, it is the first song that is not unified by a single pattern throughout in the accompaniment. In the first section (bars 1–25), the mood is one of urgency, of frustrated desire to be noticed. The repeated chord figures that rise, as though in furious protest, in bars 1–4 of the introduction evoke both heavy work, perhaps even grunting from effort, and the emphasis born of desperation, a double 'thump' on the downbeat and at mid-bar. The semiquaver figuration in bars 5–6, a linear spinning-out of all the A minor scale notes sounded in columnar form in bars 1–4, acts as a musical 'corridor' that leads to stanza 1. Schubert makes the association of the chords in bars 1–4 with work specific in his setting of the first four lines of stanza 2 when those same figures return as accompaniment to the words 'Ach, wie ist mein Arm so schwach, / Was ich hebe, was ich trage', etc. (bars 26–35); there, the chords grow softer and weaker throughout the passage. In the first section, however, Schubert gives the miller the musculature the lad so desires for his Hercules-at-the-mill feats. At the first mention of 'die schöne Müllerin' in bar 16, the music brightens to the parallel major, lasting until bar 24, for a passage filled with prosodic felicities. 'Daß', ordinarily an unstressed word, is set as a crotchet on the downbeat for emphasis (the miller longs for heroic strength *so that* the maiden will notice and admire him); in bars 79–80 near the end of the song, Schubert prolongs the word even more, carrying it over the barline to heighten its yearning quality, just as he extends the adjective 'treuen' in bar 23. The melodic and rhythmic inflection of the word 'Müllerin' in bar 20 is another example: like an archetypal lovesick youth, the miller lingers over the accented syllable in the word that represents her and then has to rush over the last two syllables in order to extend the lyrical phrase into a fifth bar.

Schubert's setting of stanza 2 is divided into three sections, each with its own figuration, mood, and tonal centre. An interior, through-composed, episodic structure is thus framed on either side by the fierce desire for the strength of a thousand.

1. bars 26–36, 'Ach, wie ist mein Arm so schwach' (A minor to C major) – Schubert translates the youth's self-mockery into an exaggeratedly athletic vocal line, the effort of lifting, hauling, cutting, and chopping made graphic in sound.

2. bars 36–45, 'Und da sitz' ich in der großen Runde' – A minor and the 'work' motive are succeeded by the clarity of C major, but even so, its quiet strains are shot through with motion in the inner voices. Schubert furthermore repeats the initial phrase transposed up a whole tone in darker D minor harmonies.

3. bars 46–59 – Here, the master speaks to oracular, full-textured F major chords (weight equals authority), reaching down to bottom F, the lowest note of the fortepianos of Schubert's day. Müller merely records the master's brief and all-inclusive praise without further characterization, but Schubert hints that the youth is overawed by a somewhat pompous employer. The tessitura rises in bars 52–3 when the miller sings 'und das liebe Mädchen sagt', both differentiating her words from her father's and setting the youth's longing on a higher plane. Müller places the crucial word 'allen' at the beginning of the last line of the poem in unmistakable emphasis, emphasis Schubert heightens still more. The maid says goodnight to everyone, not to the miller alone, and the lad's disappointment and longing are multiply apparent: in the prolonged high G; in the repetition of the words 'allen eine gute Nacht'; in the way in which the first Neapolitan sixth chord of the cycle in bar 56 anticipates the voice with a weak-beat *sforzando*; in the three-bar phrasing that results from the stress on 'allen', the miller lingering over her words as he does not over the law-and-order symmetry of her father's.

Schubert repeats Müller's first stanza at the end. The mingled disappointment and yearning that Schubert's youth feels when the miller's daughter bids everyone goodnight impels a renewed outbreak of longing for superhuman action. This time, the rhythmic pattern associated with the work motif from bars 1–4 and 26ff underlies much of the stanza, and the phrase 'merkte meinen, meinen [again, Schubert's repetition] treuen Sinn' is marked more emphatically than before. Having recounted that the miller's daughter has said an impartial 'Goodnight' to all, the brightness of the parallel major is no longer possible, and the need to insist that she pay heed to him is all the stronger. The words 'merkte meinen treuen Sinn' echo in descent to the depths of the postlude, until Schubert again asserts loud, tense energy in the final chords.

6. Der Neugierige – Langsam, 2/4, B major

The introduction bespeaks questioning before a word is sung, in particular, through the separation of the melodic line in bars 1 and 3 into fragments, and the ascent to high G♯, harmonized as a diminished seventh chord on the raised fourth degree of B major. The symmetrical phrase structure (2 + 2) of the introduction seems a mimicry of the act of posing a question and then answering it, if only because the harmonic open-endedness of the 'question' phrase is so strongly marked. In the instant of silence throughout the second half of bar 2 is the suspenseful wait for an answer.

Schubert rightly understood stanzas 1 and 2 as a prologue to the body of the poem, which begins with stanza 3. The raised fourth degree so prominent in the introduction and resolving to the fifth or dominant degree already spells in advance the emphasis on the dominant in the strophic setting of the first two stanzas, each ending on the dominant, and followed by large-scale tonic resolution only in stanza 3. Schubert thus makes clear in the tonal design the function of stanzas 1 and 2 as preparation for the direct address to the brook. The appoggiaturas that resolve upwards at the words 'Blume' and 'Stern' in bars 6 and 8 are questioning inflections; the youth may not wish to ask *them*, but he *is* preparing to ask the brook. The soft, neutral chords in the accompaniment to bars 5–19 tell of expression withheld, reined in until the proper moment. In a happy conjunction of formal convention and text expression, the quickened cadential rhythms at the end of the first period (bars 11–12) enliven the words 'was ich erführ' so gern' (what I would so gladly know). As in the introduction, the repeated musical strophe has a single deviation from the prevailing diatonicism, the diminished seventh chord on the crucial verb 'sagen' (speak, tell) in bar 10.

Impelled no doubt by the textual parallelism ('ich frage keine ... ich frage keinen'), Schubert repeats both vocal line and accompaniment for lines 1 and 2 of stanza 1 literally for the first two lines of stanza 2, but he varies the ending for greater intensification in bars 17–21, a matter of increased cadential rhythmic activity and Mozartian melismatic melody. When Schubert in bars 20–1 transposes a variation of the preceding vocal phrase 'Ob mich mein Herz belog' (if my heart lied to me) a fourth higher in the piano alone, this wordless echo, literally heightened, paves the way for the heartfelt plea that follows. When the dominant seventh chord on the final quaver beat of bar 21 stops short of resolution, we hear in the silence throughout bar 22 the youth steeling himself to ask if the miller maid loves him. In retrospect, one also hears in that silence a foreshadowing of the answer denied.

What follows might be described as pellucid profundity, music whose effect far outstrips its economy of means. The initial phrase, for example, consists of nothing more than tonic and dominant harmonies over a tonic pedal and the upper and lower neighbour notes to the tonic in the vocal line, but once heard, it is unlikely ever to be forgotten. From the beginning, the miller speaks to his heart, but in stanza 3, he turns even deeper inwards, and Schubert marks the transition to a second stage by these changes: of metre, from 2/4 to 3/4; of tempo, from *Langsam* to *Sehr langsam*; and of figuration. The 'Bächlein meiner Liebe' is supposedly mute, and yet Schubert composes a broken-chordal accompaniment for stanzas 3 and 5; one can hear the passage either as the brook flowing along wordlessly in the background, devoid of the human words the miller wishes, or as an expression of pure song, without pictorial elements at all. The simplicity of the passage, seemingly as clear as the water itself, is more apparent than real when one begins to account for its sophisticated details of construction, such as the semitone figure A♯–B in the first two-bar phrase (bars 23–4) that becomes the semitone figure C♯–D♮ at the start of the next phrase, producing a turn to the parallel minor for a brief moment. No two phrases are exactly alike, even when the harmonic progression and the accompaniment are the same, as in bars 23–4, 27–8; in the first phrase, it is the word 'Liebe' that Schubert emphasizes melodically and rhythmically, but when the same music recurs, it is both the words 'Eines' and '*wis* -sen' that are stressed. Furthermore, the break between the invocation 'O Bächlein meiner Liebe' and the words that follow is no longer applicable in the four-bar phrase that follows, in which Schubert's miller insists upon the words 'Eines – ein' in a way that precludes any pause. Here, Schubert uses the same prosodic pattern he would later use for the first two stanzas of 'Der Lindenbaum' from *Winterreise*, stanzas which also depict an intensely inward state of being; in both passages, the lines in iambic trimeters are set in 3/4 with the accented syllable of the first iamb prolonged and the second iamb of the second phrase set as a triplet quaver figure.

Stanza 4 is set apart by a drastic tonal stratagem and by the surprising intrusion of recitative into the lied at the word 'Ja', an especially stark contrast after the lyricism and the symmetries of stanzas 3 and 5 on either side. The effect, as Arnold Feil points out, is as if the miller suddenly spoke aloud (Feil, 62). It is clear what answer the miller lad wants, as the words 'Ja, heißt das eine Wörtchen' belong to tonic B major and end with a yearning appoggiatura, while the word 'Nein' on an unembellished downbeat impels a wrenching deceptive elision, the music veering off into the third-related sphere of G major and figures circling on either side of a C major harmony (Schubert's favourite Neapolitan relationship with the upper-lower neighbour note motive once again). The word 'Nein' furthermore is the inception of a full-textured passage, its multiple chord doublings in contrast with the brief passage of recitative just before. The piano doubles the voice, while singer and instrumentalist move in rhythmic unanimity, the better to underscore the rhythmic–metrical tensions of bars 35–41. Beginning with the second beat of bar 35, one hears bars 35–7 in 2/4, not the notated 3/4; the same is true for the repetition of the passage beginning in bar 38. In both, the word 'Nein' and then 'ein' are set apart as a separate one-beat bar unto themselves, as solitary as the state they symbolize.

The renewed invocation 'O Bächlein meiner Liebe' brings back the music of stanza 3 but with one wonderful difference. Not until the end of the poem does the miller spell out the question to which the two little words are the answer – 'Little brook, does she love me?'. In Schubert's reading, the question in bars 49–50 impels a deceptive wrench of what was formerly a completed tonic cadence in bars 29–30 (although without the dominant note in the low bass register, added when the cadence is repeated), a deflection at the word 'mich' ... 'does she love *me*?'. The miller must then repeat the question in order to end on the tonic, even in the vocal line: no longer question, but quiet declarative assertion.

7. Ungeduld – Etwas geschwind [in an autograph copy, Lebhaft], 3/4, A major

This song inaugurates a cluster of three strophic songs, symbolic, in Feil's judgement, of the lyrical impulse awakened by love (Feil, 64). In 'Ungeduld', the strophic repetitions are also the index of obsession, of a single *idée fixe* repeated over and over. For all the chromatic appoggiaturas, secondary dominants, and diminished seventh harmonies, the song is in A major throughout: the lad, with an unsatiated lover's monomaniacal fervour, sings the same tune again and again and stays in the same key. He cannot, however, stay still, and the thrumming triplet quavers are a register of incessant agitation throughout the entire song. When the miller begins to sing, his impatience also evident in the propulsive dotted rhythms, the triplets are divided between the left and right hands for a lighter texture that allows the words to come through. With the refrain and the climactic words 'Dein ist mein Herz', the triplets again dominate the right hand part but with the first fraction of the downbeat sounded only in the bass and the voice so that the accented syllables 'Dein', 'Herz', 'e - [wig]' resound clearly and forcefully. Furthermore, Schubert saturates the repeated strophe with sequences, not to modulate but to jump about restlessly within the tonic confines. There are even sequences within sequences to animate the A major single-mindedness: bars 1–3 are transposed and varied sequentially a whole tone lower in bars 4–6, while within the 1 + 2-bar phrase is a bass motive that descends sequentially. The leap of a sixth at the beginning of the first and second vocal phrases (this is also the intervallic relationship preceding the proclamation 'Dein ist mein Herz'), leaping from the dominant to the third degree of the tonic harmony, has much to do with establishing the ardent character of the music.

More than Müller, Schubert harps on the refrain, repeating it and prolonging its key words so that it consumes nearly half of the musical strophe. Müller changes poetic rhythm with a jolt at the word 'Dein', and Schubert emphasizes the shift from iambs to trochees even more strongly by prolongation and by the cessation of the successive dotted rhythms that emphasize the iambic metres of the poetry. Furthermore, the changes of harmonic rhythm in the preceding phrase in bars 17–18 ('auf jeden weißen Zettel möcht' ich's schreiben') pave the way for the proclamatory announcement that follows just after. The succession of V–I progressions creates a single 3/2 expanded bar in which the vocal line ends on beat 3 rather than beat 2, like the previous phrases. One quaver rest later, one quick intake of breath following the word 'schreiben', comes the long-awaited antecedent of 'es' ('ich*'s* schreiben', or 'ich *es* schreiben'). Schubert's miller proclaims 'Dein ist mein Herz' twice, initially to the same D♯ in the bass and the same V of V harmony first heard in bar 8, the only *forte* spot in the introduction. The second time, the proclamation sounds to an extended diminished seventh harmony throughout bars 21–2, a harmony that bespeaks momentary instability (the tritone in the vocal line is especially notable), for all the proclamatory radiance of the singer's high A. The sense of conflict called into being by the words 'Dein ist mein Herz' – she has not yet responded in kind – is evident each time he repeats the refrain. At the invocations of eternity, the miller vaults back up to the high A, re-harmonized in order to assert the harmonic strength commensurate with the words 'remain forever'.

8. Morgengruß – Mäßig, 3/4, C major

Schubert seems once again to have composed the repeated musical strophe of 'Morgengruß' with the words of stanza 1 in mind. Despite its miniature dimensions and its anchorage to C major, with no excursions to other keys, the compositional structure is wonderfully intricate. Each of the three unequal sections into which the stanza is divided (the setting of lines 1–3, or the greeting that shades into concern, bars 4–11; lines 4–5, with their anxious questioning, bars 12–15; and line 6, the resolution born of those questions, bars 16–23) draws on figures from the introduction and from the preceding section(s), but subtly so. The miller Schubert found in stanza 1 is someone who continually, anxiously, interprets what he sees and must therefore alter the script as he goes along. In the formal structure, the elements of change compete with the connecting links between sections for the listener's awareness. The divisions are articulated by the half-cadences at bars 10–11 and bar 15, with the voice poised questioningly in mid-air, followed in each instance by changes of figuration.

'Morgengruß' is a serenade that starts with a preliminary bit of rehearsal. The introduction begins with the two-bar phrase to which the lad will then sing 'Guten Morgen, schöne Müllerin', as if he were trying out the tune in his mind before uttering it aloud. He is too impatient, however, to rehearse beyond the first words of greeting, and the introduction ends with a cadential progression in bars 3–4 that is markedly less songlike than bars 1–2; the ascending intervals in the right hand are, however, scaled-down relatives of the opening leap of a sixth in bar 1. The semiquaver anacrusis at the end of bar 2, rather than a quaver upbeat, reinforces the impression of mild urgency, or the miller's haste to get on with restating bars 1–2 complete with their text. However, like a proper composer, he neatly finishes off a closed introduction in order to begin anew with the initial words of greeting.

When the words begin, the accompaniment is reduced to a single sustained chord per bar so that we may hear the words more clearly. One of the most distinctive elements of bar 1 and the first vocal phrase alike is the ascending leap of a sixth that was so prominent in 'Ungeduld', a musical emblem of desire and a link between the two songs. And yet, the declamation on repeated pitches that precedes the ardent intervallic leap and its rhythmic placement in mid-bar and on the offbeat render the phrase appropriately less intense: first words are always a trifle tentative when one is not sure of the response. Just as the words of greeting are rehearsed in the piano, so too the setting of the words 'was geschehen?', with the poignant multiple appoggiaturas on the downbeat of bar 10, is echoed by the piano, his fear that she might be displeased with him resounding after the question ends.

Even before the end of the first section, the process of intensification begins: the motion increases at bar 9, the piano doubles the voice, and the first chromaticism appears. With the second section, the motion increases still more, and the miller's fearfulness is reflected in the minor chords and descending sequence, with its *lamentoso* chromatic bass line, of bars 12–15. The harmonic progression is tailor-made to the situation in stanza 1 (it is less apt for subsequent stanzas, in particular, stanza 4, where music and text are at cross-purposes). The miller does not go anywhere, but his rooted tonal stance is obscured by the sequence, actually an extension of the dominant harmony in bars 10–11, that only seems to be en route elsewhere. For all the change of figuration and the novelty of sequential progression, the principal compositional elements – the Ab–G progression in the bass, the repeated note declamation in the vocal line, and the vocal rhythms – derive from the first section, appropriately so, as these questions proceed from the question in lines 2 and 3.

The final section is anchored firmly on C. Like Varo, the captain of the guard in Metastasio's *Ezio*, who asks himself over and over why he lingers when the empire is in mortal danger, the miller sings, 'So I must go away, so I must go away, go away'. The repetitions of the same phrase, with overlapping echoes in the piano, fix the music and the miller in place and even in time, enacting the wish stated in 'Ungeduld' when he sings the words 'Dein ist mein Herz und *soll es ewig bleiben*' again and again. Theoretically, the enchained phrase could continue into the eternity of unchanging Romantic love the miller desires. In a beautifully symbolic play of opposites, motion expresses the wish for stasis, and 'to go' really means 'to stay'. Even when he brings the repetitions to an end, he lingers on the final statement of the verb 'wiedergehen', all pretence of motion ceasing altogether. The vocal line ends on the third degree of the tonic triad E, not with closure on the root of the chord, and the piano echoes the 'wiedergehen' cadence at the end of the stanza, further confirmation of the miller's reluctance to leave and the more profound underlying desire to stop the clock. Most telling of all, Schubert rhythmically re-casts the melody of the initial words of greeting, this time with the leap of a sixth culminating on the downbeat as in 'Ungeduld', more ardent than the first phrase of the song. 'My end is my beginning' indeed in 'Morgengruß', but the ending is transformed.

9. Des Müllers Blumen – Mäßig, 6/8, A major

Schubert begins 'Des Müllers Blumen' with an enigmatic gesture that he would use again in his second Müller cycle. From a single sustained unharmonized octave in the bass, mysterious because devoid of explanatory context, the notes of the tonic triad rise two octaves. Four years later, a similar gesture, in the same metre and tonality, is the musical corridor from waking reality back to the dream-world of 'Frühlingstraum' from *Winterreise*, in which the wanderer finds refuge from sorrow in beautiful dreams of reciprocated love. The resemblance goes beyond coincidence. The miller in 'Des Müllers Blumen' maintains a brief equipoise by dwelling momentarily in a daydream, a fantasy land he can dispose to his liking. He is as yet more fortunate than the protagonist of the later cycle, however; there are no ravens screeching on the roof to awaken him and no apprehension of sorrow.

'Des Müllers Blumen' is the point of least tension in the cycle. Schubert duly noted the words 'Der Bach der ist des Müllers Freund' and made the relationship of the piano and the voice a symbolic indicator of the friendship. The miller adopts the brook's arpeggiated voice; the right hand part and the voice mostly flow in the same direction, at times diverging briefly in contrary motion. As in 'Ungeduld' (but more calmly), the stanza stays in A major throughout, with only a few chromatic inflections. The miller once again pursues a single idea, if reflectively this time. But however quietly, he still insists that the miller's daughter is his: 'Drum sind es meine Blumen'. As in 'Ungeduld', the climactic assertion is marked by a rhythmic shift from iambs to trochees, by the downbeat on the word 'Drum' ('Darum', therefore), followed by an additional mid-bar downbeat on the word 'sind', and by the shift from the two-bar phrases to three-bar phrases. The miller's logic is questionable, and Schubert underscores the warped reasoning when his miller prolongs the word 'therefore', as if emphasis alone could make it so. The statement that the flower-blue eyes are his impels one of the only registers of disturbance in an otherwise placid song: the deceptive deflection at bar 18, a commonplace of antecedent–consequent phrases but one with an additional resonance here.

This is the only song in the cycle that simply stops at the final syllable of text, without even the minimal running-down of the accompanimental figuration that one finds at the end of 'Wohin?' or 'Halt!'. 'Des Müllers Blumen' thus ends with the word 'weinen' still resonant in the air. As the fantasy-tears of this song are followed by real tears in 'Tränenregen', Schubert pairs the two songs, in part by omitting any postlude from 'Des Müllers Blumen' and beginning 'Tränenregen' with a seemingly unprepared dissonance. Actually, the dissonance *is* prepared, if unconventionally so, by the manner in which 'Des Müllers Blumen' ends.

10. Tränenregen – Ziemlich langsam, 6/8, A major

The metre and tonality are the same as 'Des Müllers Blumen', as is the unceasing quaver motion, but the simplicity of that song is no longer possible. With the release of desire in 'Tränenregen', forms and beings begin to dissolve, and the longing for death, ill-concealed by passion, impels weeping.

'Tränenregen' begins with a beautiful and distinctive compound of gestures in the introduction. Schubert, I believe, saw that the miller speaks in the past tense throughout and that his knowledge of the vignette's ending colours its rendition from the very beginning. With the upbeat to bar 1, we hear what Edward Cone, referring to the sixth *Moment Musical*, has called a 'promissory note', a chromatic disturbance that foreshadows later events in the unfolding musical structure.[7] The raised fifth degree E♯ in the inner voice produces, in conjunction with the bass and soprano pitches, an augmented tonic harmony which is, despite the *pianissimo* dynamics, violent in its unconventionality as the initial simultaneity of a composition. In eighteenth- and early-nineteenth-century music, augmented chords are most often the result of passing motion; here, the chord implies a passageway from 'Des Müllers Blumen' to 'Tränenregen', a bridge interrupted and displaced to another register when the scene changes. (Although not every occurrence of the augmented tonic chord in the body of the song is so perfectly calibrated to the poetry, the harmony invests the word 'Wir', or 'we', at the end of bar 4 with the appropriate tension.) The linear motive E♯–F♯–E♮ is re-harmonized in the second half of the repeated strophe as the cadential articulation on the III chord (C♯ major) in bar 18 at the words 'die Sternlein hinter*drein*', linking the two halves by means of similar voice-leading; but ultimately, the 'promissory note' of 'Tränenregen' is revealed as the sixth scale-degree of the parallel minor (F♮) in the final stanza. Throughout the repeated strophes (stanzas 1–6), Schubert insists upon the third degree of the major mode (C♯) by placing it as an appoggiatura, its resolution delayed, in the soprano at the beginnings of phrases and resolves the chromatic disturbance in the inner voice upwards to F♯. But with the final stanza, F resolves downwards to the fifth degree and C supplants C♯. And yet, the key signature does not change, and Schubert attempts to reassert A major, with its raised third and sixth degrees, in the final stanza (the diminished seventh chord on D♯ in bar 30 contains notes from both major and minor modes). Somewhat fancifully, one can hear the promissory note and its consequences as analogous to the operations of memory, self-deception, and truth in the poem. The miller knows the sad ending from the start and defends himself against the knowledge; its tension imbues even the repeated strophes, but ultimately becomes an irresistible force in the final stanza.

The introduction thus both foretells what is to come and begins the process of denial. The harmonic tensions are greatest at the start of each one-bar unit and are then diffused in the descending, 'falling tears' motion throughout the bar. The emphasis of a dissonant simultaneity on the upbeat and an accent on the downbeat of each bar of the introduction blurs the metrical outlines as tears blur what one sees. Above all, Schubert foretells, in the motivic relationships and overlapping inexact echoes between the three voices, the images of reflection to follow in the poem. The scalewise intervallic figures of a third turn over and around, sway back and forth, in a melodic chain that hovers, until bar 4, just short of anchorage on the tonic, while the blurring of metrical pulses induced by the rhythmic overlapping of the voices is the corollary to an indistinct nocturnal world in which fantasies of intimacy can – briefly – flourish.

Müller's rhyme-repetitions of 'beisammen – zusammen' in stanza 1 perhaps inspired Schubert to double the vocal line in the piano throughout much of the song, the two thus a symbolically charged concord of paired entities. (We are all the more aware of the doubling when the piano lags slightly behind, then catches up, as in bar 10, or when there is neighbour-note motion in the piano that bridges two vocal phrases, as in bar 6.) The doubling breaks apart, one notices, when the miller recounts the maiden's parting gibe ('Es kommt ein Regen') and then resumes for the final vocal phrase (bars 31–2, 'Ade, ich geh' nach Haus'). Even as he repeats her words of departure, the miller denies their import and asserts once again the dream of tonal union.

As we have seen, Müller's poem is made up of paired quatrains, each pair linked by its own thematic element, followed by a single stanza that is both the consequence and the destruction of what precedes it. The spell the lad casts on himself is all of a piece: his desire calls the maiden's eyes forth from her body in stanza 4, submerges the heavens in the brook in stanza 5, and sings of death in stanza 6. Schubert, who recognized the poetic strategy, sets stanzas 1–6 as a strophic song, an encapsulated lyric structure enclosed by double bars whose significance is symbolic as well as formal. Each pair of quatrains becomes a musical strophe divided into symmetrical halves, each half ending with a piano interlude that is the voice of the brook. The first occurrence of the interlude is elided with the cadence on the dominant E major at the words 'hinab in den rieselnden Bach' (down below in the laughing brook); later, E major is the tonality of 'Des Baches Wiegenlied', when the lad is indeed 'down below' in a brook that no longer finds cause for laughter. But the boundaries that contain the repeated strophes are no longer possible for the setting of stanza 7, the undoing of the spell, the solitary verse that overflows the bounds of stanzas 1–6 as tears spill from the miller's eyes. In a wonderfully subtle compositional analogy to events in the poetry, the final section is a 'Spiegel so kraus' of the song that precedes it.

Schubert ignores the prosy flatness of the miller maid's disenchanting words at the end. Rather, it is the miller's melancholy, his tears clouding the song, his tension given musical life in the chromatic ascent throughout bars 28–30, and his attempt to reinstate the illusion of *Traulichkeit* that we hear. When he recounts her departure ('Ade, ich geh' nach Haus') to a variant of the A major cadence with which he concludes each of the repeated strophes, one can only hear it as a desperately-willed contradiction of the words: where she sunders even the simulacrum of togetherness, he refuses assent and instead sings her parting shot to his own music of illusory intimacy. Even more telling, Schubert does not end the song with the tonic chord in the middle of bar 32, nor even pause there. Since the miller is unwilling to acknowledge the finality of her actions, Schubert returns seamlessly to the music of the initial bars of the introduction (bars 1–2), with not a note altered; but tears well up again, this time wordlessly, and the postlude slips into A minor (a key associated elsewhere in Schubert's *oeuvre* with solitary, tragic beings such as Mignon and the Harper), which finally, softly, conquers the A major of the repeated strophe. By the end, one hears the struggle to maintain A major as heroic, tragically so.

11. **Mein!** – Mäßig geschwind, alla breve, D major

As he would do later with 'Die Post' in *Winterreise*, Schubert galvanizes the cycle at mid-point, infusing it with fresh energy after the melancholy ending of 'Tränenregen'. Here, he does so by recalling 'Das Wandern', not as literal reminiscence but in the similar two-beat stresses in each bar, emphasized all the more by the downbeat accents and sustained minims in the bass and inner voices; in the similarity of motion, the alternation between tonic and dominant harmonies for much of the introduction, and the athletic character of the vocal line in the A sections of this three-part form, or what Feil calls 'yodel melodics' (Feil, 68). 'Mein!', however, is far more exuberant than 'Das Wandern'.

Müller's miller staggers from line to line in delusional transport, but Schubert's miller, a healthier creature, dances for joy. All of the elements established at the beginning – the regular rhythmic patterns and the melodic *Schwung*, especially the rising triadic phrases that swing upwards sequentially in bars 9–14 – override the complexities of Müller's verse, straightening out the poet's wavering line lengths and changeable metres. Everything is subordinated to the impulses of musical joy, which regularizes whatever it encounters and converts it into dance, as in the emphatic trochaic rhythms of the phrase in bars 30–7 ('Die geliebte Müllerin ist mein, ist mein'). One would not ordinarily place so much emphasis on the definite article, but here, merely accurate prosody is bent to the strong metrical and rhythmic patterns and the roller-coaster arpeggiated vocal line. The strenuousness of the vocal part, coupled with the unusual amount of repetition, tell of exultation that is perhaps exaggerated but real; Schubert's miller truly believes that the girl has looked on him with favour and rejoices in music untainted by Müller's suggestions of delusion. In bars 24–5 and 28–9 at the words 'Schalle heut' ein Reim allein' (the meadows, or 'Haine', and the verb 'schallen', 'to ring out', must have inspired the open-air perfect fifths reiterated throughout bars 22–9), Schubert sets the definite article 'ein' properly on a weak beat but also on a high note emphasized still more by the octave leap. Only one rhyme will do, and it practically leaps off the page in its exuberance.

The fourfold insistence that she 'is mine, is mine' in bars 36–40 culminates in a turn to the warmth of flat submediant for the middle section (Schumann does likewise, to similar effect, in his setting of Friedrich Rückert's 'Widmung', Op. 25, no. 1). In the suddenness of the modulation, beginning with the first F♮ in the piano at the beginning of bar 38, Schubert makes us hear the precise moment when delight is overtaken by a flood of warmth. With the change of key comes the change to a more declamatory style in the vocal part, especially the questioning upwards inflection and the naturalistic rests after the invocations 'Frühling' and 'Sonne', although the accompanimental patterns from the A section continue their joyous pulsations throughout the entire song. And yet, a sense of disbelief in his luck, the fear that he might become 'ganz allein', represses the exuberance and tempers his joy with minor inflections. Taking his cue from Müller, whose last line unfurls to lengths emblematic of the wide world, Schubert prolongs both the prefix 'un -' in the key word 'unverstanden' and the phrase to which it belongs. The Db chromatic neighbour-note of the prefix is especially expressive after all of the preceding D♮s.

Schubert returns to D major in the piano interlude in bars 60–3 and then repeats the setting of the first nine lines almost unchanged, with only the final vocal cadence altered. The formal reasons are certainly compelling – he has to bring the miller home to D after his excursion in a non-tonic 'weite Welt' – but the compositional decision is psychologically revealing as well. Schubert's miller, unlike Müller's character, casts off all traces of self-doubt and returns to the unalloyed joy of the beginning, there to dance with delight once more. In Schubert's reading, the maiden *is* kind in some fashion, however superficial and however brief, and the pathos of the whole cycle is deepened by the contrast between the exultation of 'Mein!' and the tragedy that follows.

12. Pause – Ziemlich geschwind, 4/4, Bb major

'I have hung my lute on the wall', the miller says, but Schubert assigns the idea of the lute (the ability to create music) to the piano, separate from the miller's musings in the vocal line. 'Pause' begins with an unusually lengthy and self-contained introduction, an eight-bar period in a tidy antecedent–consequent structure that ends with an equally tidy authentic cadence, the passage utterly diatonic. Four times in the introduction, one hears the same one-bar motive; when it starts up again in bar 9, the miller begins to sing – *after* the resumption of the instrumental figures and thus distinct from them. Music is now something apart from the miller-musician, bereft by distress of the ability to create, and Schubert suggests the separation by means of an introduction entirely instrumental in nature, that is, devoid of text representation. Eduard Hanslick himself, that arbiter of the absolute ideal, could not have devised a better textbook symbol of 'pure music' than the lute-piano of 'Pause'. Without actually composing uninspired music,

Schubert suggests that invention is at a low ebb in these neatly boxed-in phrases with their limited harmonies and small intervallic steps, and his miller is disturbed by the fact. When he sings, he attempts an infusion of lyric energy with the leaps of a sixth in bars 9–10 and bars 12–13, then tries to conform to the lute song, so that the singer and his instrument may once again be paired as two parts of a whole, but without complete success. Even where the miller mimics the lute's rhythms and borrows its melodic contours, the two remain distinct, as in the motivic figure in mirror image and contrary motion one finds in bars 15–16 ('Ich kann nicht mehr singen, mein Herz ist zu voll'), perturbation conveyed in up-and-down, to-and-fro motion within a small space.

This is where the cycle first flowers into tragedy. When the miller recalls 'the burning sorrow of my desire', sorrow he *could* express in song, Schubert shifts, with no preliminary ado, to G minor harmonies and varies the previous motive of a scalewise third as a flowing tears figure (one first finds it in Schubert's setting of Goethe's 'Wonne der Wehmut' of 1815, beginning with the words 'Trocknet nicht, trocknet nicht, / Tränen der ewigen Liebe!') in both the voice and the piano, symbolic of the singer and his lute as they were once joined together. The composer even activates the half-cadences in bars 23 and 29 with the rising scalewise bass figure in dotted rhythms that he later uses in the still more tragic context of 'Der Wegweiser' in *Winterreise*. But he does not stay in G minor and in tears: the sorrow the miller invokes here is not yet real, but rather the material from which to fashion songs. Thus, the consequent phrases shift to major harmonies and the kind of wide-ranging, arpeggiated melodic writing emblematic of song from the beginning. Here, the miller senses, with dread, the nearness of grief beyond bearing; the lute-piano, in its wordless echo of the words 'Leiden wär' nicht klein' in bar 32, prolongs the pitch to which we have just heard the word 'nicht' (not) on the offbeat, the rhythmic imbalance constituting still further emphasis and underscoring the sense of disturbance. The echo, with its overtones of mockery, is multivalent: one hears in the prolongation of 'not' both the fear that the coming sorrow will indeed be 'not small' and the wish for negation – 'May it *not* be so'.

The 'great burden of his fortune', its weight evident in the thick *fortissimo* chords, presses the harmonies momentarily into lower, flatter, darker realms and banishes the songlike contours of bars 21–32. 'Glückes Last' on a Db major chord is a tritone distant from the G minor of 'Meiner Sehnsucht allerheißesten Schmerz', as far apart as can be. The miller wonders why 'no sound on earth' comes to mind (the expression 'kein Klang auf Erden' conveys how deeply disturbed he is by the banishment of his art); for lack of any other sound, he takes the lute's figures and the motifs of his sorrowing song and attempts to make something else of them, but literally becomes stuck. This time, when the piano echoes the words 'in sich faßt?' in bars 40–1, the dotted rhythmic pattern gives the repetition an extra urgency. In the bare dominant triad of Schubert's bar 41, one can almost see the miller frozen in denial, refusing to move beyond the question to an answer he does not want to hear. The chord simply stretches, motionless, throughout the bar.

The miller returns to the instrumental lute-music of the beginning, an abbreviated return but otherwise little changed. He is determined at first to resign himself to the circumstances of the moment, but the pressure of underlying tensions makes the equipoise of resignation impossible to maintain. Song style gives way abruptly to a brief outburst of *recitativo accompagnato* and a line that rises steeply in fear, then stops in mid-air on a prolonged C minor chord. The tonality of C minor will shortly, in 'Der Jäger', again be associated with fear and panic, fear given a name and a face.

What follows after the fermata in bar 55 is an unforgettable rupture with any classical notions of song form. In Schubert's reading of the poem, an unknown lapse of time occurs between the shudders of fear in line 14 and the question 'Warum ließ ich das Band auch hängen *so lang* [italics mine]?' in line 15. Schubert renders the passage of time in terms of tonal distance: a mere four bars after the temporal plane set in Bb major, we are transported to the distant and darker chord of Ab, a chromatic thief in the night that appears as if from nowhere and becomes a paradoxically non-tonicized 'tonic' in bars 56–62. That is, the lute figure from bars 1ff is repeated over and over on an Ab harmony, but nothing else is done to establish Ab major as a new tonic. Those seven bars are remarkably static, a suspenseful walking-in-place: what will follow such a blatant harmonic oddity, such a disturbance in the order of things? The startling speed with which the chromatic intruder (all the more bizarre for being in major mode) appears and the way it lies there like a stone, once present, are indeed eerie in effect.

At the end, the miller asks himself whether the Aeolian harp sound of the wind on the lute strings is the 'echo of love's suffering or the prelude to new songs', words that reveal the strategy of self-deception at the heart of this poem. The old songs have, he tells us, been impelled by love's sorrow and the new songs that lurk just around the corner will arise from even worse pangs. But the miller only seems to be probing the levels below conscious awareness in an attempt to make them yield their secrets;

actually, he is staving off unhappy knowledge. He cannot banish it, however, so he asks the same question over in different words without ever permitting himself to go farther, to an answer. Schubert makes the extreme tension of the psychic deception musically apparent in the unconventionality of each stage of the descent by flat submediant progressions: C minor to Ab to Fb. The final question, haunted by an answer the miller knows but cannot bring himself to say, cuts too close to the bone, and the poem ends. Silence is the only evasion left for the poet's miller after *these* words. Schubert, however, fundamentally alters the poet's implications at the end when he turns suddenly from the uneasily prolonged Fb major harmony and recitative style back to tonic (the tritone relationship of Fb and Bb recalls the tritone relationship between the G minor beginning of the B section and its Db major goal) and arpeggiated song style at the words 'Soll es das Vorspiel neuer Lieder sein?' Schubert's miller tries to establish the 'neue Lieder' in bars 67–9 as lyrical, hopeful strains – 'yodel melodics' in the key of 'Das Wandern' – entirely unlike the 'echo of my love's suffering'. Twice, he states the contrasting tonal gestures, as if to emphasize the dissimilar harmonic strategies, but without a response to his question. As in bar 41, the tonic chords in bars 69 and 77 stretch quiescently throughout the bar. When Schubert brings back the lute figuration of bars 5–8 as the postlude, he sets the seal on the lack of an answer, on the miller's refusal to confront what lies around the corner. His character goes back to the beginning and repeats the neutral strains that evoke neither joy nor sorrow.

13. Mit dem grünen Lautenbande – Mäßig, 2/4, Bb major

The sustained Bb major chord at the beginning of 'Mit dem grünen Lautenbande' foreshadows the similarly enigmatic introduction to his later setting of Heine's 'Ihr Bild' and evokes an encoded significance by its isolation. Einstein, offended by the mysteriousness of the gesture, recommended that it be omitted in performance, thus bringing the paired songs closer together. Justifying the deletion, he observed that the miller at the end of 'Pause' asks uneasily if the wind sighing across the lute strings is 'the prelude to new songs'; with the initial chord removed, the 'new song' that follows is the miller maid's.[8] His suggestion that the chord is a disposable extension of the twelfth song hardly seems admissible nowadays, although Einstein *did* strike to the heart of the matter. The chord is indeed an extension of 'Pause': in fact, the entirety of 'Mit dem grünen Lautenbande' can be heard as an extension of the previous song, an interlude before the 'new songs of love's sorrow' begin with 'Der Jäger'. The first chord is not, however, disposable. Schubert frames the introduction on either side with enigmatic gestures, as there is a fermata-prolonged rest following the root-position tonic chord in bar 3, the conclusion of a phrase whose diatonicism and rhythmic insouciance is a musical portrait of the miller maid. The compositional elements in the introduction suggest a miniature *mise-en-scène*. At the beginning, the miller is alone with his questions from the end of 'Pause', the tonic chord frozen in place. The longer the chord is sustained, the more one is aware of the passage of time and the futility of any attempt to remain fixed in place and fixed in time. Too long and the sustained chord is unbearable, like the miller's predicament. The maiden then enters the scene, perhaps humming to herself, and notices the green ribbon; struck by the sight, she pauses and stares at it before speaking. The miller, remembering the moment, starts from the beginning with the unspoken fear of the future and desire for stasis at the end of 'Pause'.

The two voices in the first stanza were clearly the inspiration for the bipartite design of the musical strophe, each half ending with the refrain 'ich hab'/du hast das Grün so gern'; in the first half, we hear the maiden's song, in the second half the lad's response based on her figures. The design is not so apt for the succeeding two stanzas, although the prevailing diatonicism bespeaks the miller's wish to echo the maiden's song as well as her every whim. Feil describes her music as 'friendly', and it is indeed graceful, elegant, buoyant, in Schubert's best quasi-Mozartian manner, if devoid of deeper feeling (Feil, 70). In several of Schubert's compositional choices, we hear the miller maid as she is, the miller who reports her words as sweetness-and-light become sound, and the composer. For example, we hear the miller's voice, even as he sings what are ostensibly her words and tune, in bar 7, where Schubert again refers to 'Pause'. The fermata-prolonged harmonic articulation on the D major chord (V of G minor) at the end of the second texted phrase ('an der Wand') is the echo of his experience in 'Pause', not hers. And yet, throughout the first half, Schubert stays poised on the dividing line between grace and a near-parody of sweetness, diatonic to a fault. It is possible, for example, to hear the parodic touch in such details as the dotted pattern in the piano at bar 9, the pianist enlivening the word 'gern' even more (this is already a wonderfully buoyant gesture because of the ascent to the high F on the offbeat).

When the lad himself speaks in his own voice in bars 12–19, he adopts her first two phrases but makes them more resolute, the boldness stemming in part from the octave leaps. Schubert pokes gentle fun at the lad's eagerness to do as she wishes when the quaver syllabic declamation gives way to semiquaver motion at the words 'knüpf' ich's ab und [send' es dir]', a prosodic rush to do her bidding that leads to a cadence on the dominant. The music as well is sent to another place nearby. Furthermore, the arrival on F and the word 'dir' impel quickened motion in the piano and ascent two octaves higher. With the refrain at the end of stanza 1 ('Nun hab' das Grüne gern') in bars 16–17, the miller speaks to the maiden and does so in her treble, feminine sphere first before coming back down to the original level.

14. Der Jäger – Geschwind, 6/8, C minor

Schubert uses the fortepiano as a true percussion instrument for this hunting song with a difference. He would not have known that the equation between canonic imitation and the hunt goes back to the *caccias* of Trecento Italy, but he understood that the miller wishes to chase the hunter away, to hunt the huntsman himself, and signifies that desire by means of a significantly brief imitative passage, confined to the intro-duction/interlude/postlude. Schubert, I believe, saw and registered the psychological complexity of the poem: his miller wants to chase away the hunter, but feels himself unable to do so and therefore does not continue the imitative hunt beyond the span of two bars. And yet, the wish recurs, the chase flaring up whenever the words cease and then merging into the hammered pulsations that prevail throughout the song.

The *martellato* writing in 'Der Jäger' can be found nowhere else in the cycle; the very look of the printed page is different from every other song in *Die schöne Müllerin*. Each bar has two stresses filled in with an insistent pulse on almost every quaver beat; in bar 3, rather than sustaining down-beats for a crotchet, Schubert repeats the initial quaver, filling the air with the staccato pulsations of panic. The sound-and-fury is remarkably stark, the three-voice texture a departure from the multiple chord-tone dou-blings characteristic of Schubert's rich sound. The vocal part is doubled throughout in the piano but at the unison, the effect unlike the superficially similar doubling in 'Tränenregen'. Here it is steely reinforcement for the singer's melody. The introduction and many of the subsequent phrases in the body of the song begin or end with perfect intervals, yet another means of emphasis; the entire song ends when all three voices in the accom-paniment converge on the unharmonized tonic pitch.

The symmetry of the vocal phrases, their brevity, and the literal phrase-repetition are perfect for the temper of the song: the lad spits out these adrenaline-driven phrases without any leeway for breadth or breath, while literal repetition constitutes furious emphasis. (The headlong motion in 6/8 and the staccato touch throughout are reminiscent of the earlier setting of Goethe's 'An Schwager Kronos', D. 369.) The corrosive emotions in this poem run roughshod over such niceties as inflected prosody; the omission of the commas in line 2 by Sauer & Leidesdorf's engravers ('Bleib trotziger Jäger in deinem Revier') in the first edition seems only appropriate to the syllabic rush of notes paired with Müller's rush of words. The effort required to enunciate the clustered plosive consonants in this text at a rapid tempo makes apparent the difficulty of such thoughts, especially as the vocal part is constricted by the gasping breaths that are all the singer has time to take between phrases. Schubert does not indicate a single rest in the vocal part: not only is this a visual emblem of the way in which such poisonous jealousy stifles the breath, but he thereby forces the singer to enact some of the physical manifestations of jealous rage. The brusque cadence with which each eight-bar subsection of the strophe ends makes all the more obvious the way in which the miller's angry thoughts tumble one after another in breathless haste. Upon hearing a strong cadence in early-nineteenth-century music, one expects a minimal amount of breathing room before the next succession of events, but that is never the case in 'Der Jäger'.

Müller follows a ten-line stanza, already an index of verbose anger, with a twelve-line stanza, the miller's fury spilling over into an extra two lines. Schubert, however, who understood the two stanzas as alike in their design (the miller bidding the hunter begone, then advising him how to please the miller maid), sets them to the same musical strophe, unchanged in the service of repetitive emphasis. Schubert's miller therefore repeats lines 9 and 10 of stanza 1 (the injunction to the hunter to shave/to become civilized lest he frighten the maiden) to the same four-bar phrase, the concomitant in music to the repeated verbal bludgeons hurled in a fit of anger. In fact, exact phrase-repetition dominates the strophe, with its three subsections of eight bars each.

One of the most remarkable aspects of the song is foreshadowed in the appearance both of Bb and B♮ in the introduction and in the stressed pitches C and Eb at the beginning of the introduction. The miller alternates between cadences on C minor and cadences on Eb major that follow in close proximity, tonal symbols of his vacillation between imperious orders to the hunter to leave and his own wrought-up misery, of the struggle for primacy between the miller and the hunter. Eb is of course a horn tonality, identified with the hunter, and the vocal part throughout recalls an assemblage of horn-call tattoos and hunting signals, but not as literal quotation. The miller angrily attempts to define territory 'für dich, für mich' and therefore steps back and forth in tight, short steps between two closely related planes. He and the hunter are now akin, linked by their attraction to the miller maid, and move within the same circle (but not, one notices, parallel modes with a shared tonic). This alternation between the raised and the natural (Bb) forms of the seventh degree of the C minor scale is an important element of the subsequent two sections as well, especially in the second section (bars 13–20), with its distinctive chromatic descent in the inner voice and the percussive repeated pitches in the topmost voice. The linear chromaticism has, for those familiar with other Schubert songs, an additional resonance of death, here of murderous fantasies. To cite only one example, in his setting of Johann Mayrhofer's powerful poem 'Auf der Donau' (On the Danube), D. 558 of 1817, the words 'Wellen drohn wie Zeiten Untergang' (Waves, like time, threaten doom) culminate in a lengthy chromatic descent, 'Untergang' (to go under, or doom) made graphic. With each section of 'Der Jäger', the ceiling rises: the apex of the first section is C, the second section Eb, and the third section G, outlining the tonic triad. From beginning to end of each strophe, the pitch of panic and fury literally ascends. When Schubert's miller shouts 'die *E* - ber' (the boars) on a climactic high G, then plunges downward an octave to '*Jäger* - held', he underlines unforgettably Müller's equation between the huntsman and the wild animals most emblematic of inhuman savagery.

15. Eifersucht und Stolz – Geschwind, 2/4, G minor–major

The brook's swift, frothing motion is a metaphor for the tumult in the miller's mind and heart, tumult artfully mirrored in the complexities of this song. In the 'curling' ('kraus') contours of the introduction, one notices particularly the emphatic downbeat beginning, the perfect fifth sounded over and over in the left hand (the initial bars of 'Gretchen am Spinnrade' come to mind, with its similarly incessant, curly motion in the right hand and hollow fifths in the left hand), and the semitone motive F♯ – G at the topmost level of the broken chords in the right hand. That same semitone cell later becomes the wrenching cries of pain 'Kehr um, kehr um!' an octave higher, the tonic pitch shifted emphatically to the down-beat. When the singer enters, the emotional turbulence engenders restless tonal motion. Each of the first three phrases ends in a different place harmonically from its beginning, not modulation but rather tonal 'rushing about' in which the directive 'Kehr um' cleverly 'turns back' to tonic G minor. (One notes the interval of the diminished fourth, traditionally associated with lamentation, twice in the singer's first two bars.) The fourth phrase is a repetition of the third; as in 'Der Jäger', with which these two phrases (bars 12–22) share similar descending, parallel first inversion chords as a pathway for tonal motion, anger takes the form of literal phrase repetition – of an asymmetrical five-bar phrase. The 'schnell' dotted rhythms of the singer's four-bar phrases ('Wohin so schnell, so kraus und wild . . . eilst du voll Zorn dem frechen Bruder') are augmented in the five-bar phrases, the singer prolonging the directive to return and the adjectives '*ihr*en *lei*chten' (her flighty). The interpretive emphasis on '*ihr*en' is especially forceful because of the bright -i vowel after the darker closed -u of 'Kehr *um*'. Everything about the prosody compels admiration: the leap of a sixth, bypassing the tonic pitch, that energizes the initial question 'Wohin'; the prolongation of the second, usually weaker syllable of 'lie - ber' so that the words 'my *dear* brook' acquire the proper angry emphasis; the syncopated rise that gives the word 'Jä - ger' a vengeful kick; the gasping breaths mandated in 'Kehr um, (rest), kehr um, (rest), und schilt erst deine Müllerin' . . . and the list goes on.

The miller in anguish hammers the G minor cadence over and over as he repeats 'Kehr um, kehr um, kehr um'. At bars 25–6, Schubert varies the semiquaver motion in the right hand to insist upon the pitches of the Bb harmonies to follow and the bagpipe-like turning figures that accompany the children's songs and dances the miller invokes near the end. Here, the miller 'speaks', the first four bars of his long, angry question in lines 5 and 6 mostly declaimed on a single pitch; the effect of the subsequent prolonged syllables (especially the rhyming vowels of '*lan* - gem *Hal* - se'), octave leap downwards, and unbalanced five-bar phrase in bars 31–5 is therefore all the greater. The neck, the phrase, and the melody are indeed stretched to exaggerated and expressive lengths.

In angry reproach, Schubert's miller repeats Müller's lines 7 and 8 ('Wenn von dem Fang der Jäger lustig zieht nach Haus, / da steckt kein sittsam Kind den Kopf zum Fenster 'naus'). Here, the brook no longer rushes onwards in semiquavers, the sound of horn-call fanfares fills the air, and the miller again resorts to percussive, syllabic declamation in equal quavers, as in 'Der Jäger'. The multiple -t's, -s's, and -k's of the principal clause in line 8, hard to enunciate at this tempo, again bespeak the difficulty of the thought, reminiscent of similar difficulties in the previous song. The hunter's merry music (line 7), momentarily in the relative major key belonging to the world of Nature, ascends, while the subsequent reproach to the miller maid (line 8) descends to the minor and the tragic key of the present moment.

Within a song whose every detail of formal proportion is considered, Schubert wonderfully conveys the immediacy of emotional life, a sense of the mental process by which one thought leads to the next. In bars 50–3, the cadence with which the reproachful words in line 8 end is elided with the return to the brook and the directive 'Geh', Bächlein, hin und sag' ihr das'. The thought occurs to him so quickly that there is no pause between lines 8 and 9, barely time for the singer to take a gasping breath before the verb in the imperative 'Geh'' – sung as a semiquaver upbeat! 'Hurry, don't waste any time about it', the music insists, brightening to the parallel major at the thought of action, even through an intermediary. Similarly, Schubert registers the exact time, that is, the instant *before* words emerge, at which the miller is struck by the need to temper his directive with qualifications about withheld information: the right hand continues to spin out a G major chord in bar 55, as if in suspended animation, and the bass remains fixed, the music pausing in place. From here to the change of key signature in bar 67, Schubert varies the prosody of his two- and four-bar vocal phrases in accord with the changing word rhythms and emotional temper of the text in a manner both wonderfully controlled in compositional technique and wonderfully free in effect. 'Doch sag ihr nicht' is quickly declaimed, leading to the downbeat on the crucial word 'nicht'; for the words 'hörst du, kein Wort', Schubert this time places the verb in the imperative on the downbeat and prolongs it slightly, then inserts the quickest of breaths before 'kein Wort' for emphasis. The adjective 'traurigen' in the next phrase is elongated even further and darkened to the mediant minor, the self-pitying miller lingering for an instant on his sadness. As in bars 55–6, the music runs in place in bars 65–6, the words 'Sag ihr' prolonged while the miller considers what the brook must say, since it cannot tell the truth. It is truly a feat of compositional virtuosity by which Schubert mimics the motions of a mind in turmoil and does so within a formal structure of impeccable design.

The lie requires a mask, a change of face, hence the change of key signature. Schubert renders the pained self-mockery of the music for children – childish strains for those young and deluded enough to think love is possible – as an almost parodistically folkish melody and bagpipe figures in the piano. But misery erupts through the assumed lightheartedness in outbursts of G minor, all the more violent for their brevity. (Later, in 'Mut' from *Winterreise*, Schubert would similarly distinguish between truth and misery in minor mode and feigned merriment in major.) At the end, the earlier cries 'Kehr um, kehr um' (bars 22–4) return but *in major mode* (Sag ihr's), by now as tragic as minor.

16. Die liebe Farbe – Etwas langsam, 2/4, B minor

Schubert sets 'Die liebe Farbe' in the B minor tonality that Beethoven once called 'the black tonality', the key of the most intense mournfulness, and sounds an incessant funeral tocsin on F♯ throughout the three stanzas of this strophic song. Accordingly, the harmonic palette is restricted to B minor, B major, dominant, and relative major chords only. One thinks of the compositional restrictions, even more drastic, that Schubert later imposed on himself in 'Der Leiermann' at the end of *Winterreise*, a song of similar death-haunted alienation originally in the same tonality.

For Schubert, the changes of tone from one stanza to the next in Müller's poem are subsumed under the pervasive solemnity of the moment. The subtleties that belie the seeming simplicity of the song begin with the five bar introduction/postlude that frames each stanza, a passage for the piano alone that establishes elements of the texted body of the song and yet is distinct from it. The funeral tocsin begins with a low bass B on the downbeat; the initial strong beat contributes at the start to the solemn atmosphere. That sustained bass pitch is then joined by the right hand, setting in motion the death-knell that only stops at the end of the song, tolling throughout introduction and stanza alike. Four years later, Schubert would again sound a stream of non-legato repeated pitches throughout 'Gute Nacht' and much of 'Der Wegweiser', the first and twentieth songs in *Winterreise*, where the figures can be heard as the musical symbol of the wanderer's journey. Here in the introduction to 'Die liebe Farbe', however, one hears the continual semiquaver pulse as separable into anacrusis figures, reinforced by motion in the bass, that culminate in the accented chordal appoggiaturas on the downbeat of bars 2, 3, and 4, followed by brief moments of stasis that extend the chord of resolution. The chordal appoggiatura at the exact midpoint of the introduction, on the downbeat of bar 3, however, does not resolve until the end of the introduction, and the delayed resolution seems a small-scale symbol of pain that lingers without surcease. The passage is markedly richer in texture than the song proper, especially in bar 4, and the effect when the voice enters is therefore one of tragic diminishment.

With the first words, the low register disappears until the culmination of the refrain, as if the ground had vanished from beneath the miller's feet. There are, for a time, no deeper bass tones to compete with the singer; the texture thins to the ostinato in the inner voice, the vocal line, and a 'bass' line that doubles the voice rhythmically throughout and, much of the time, melodically in parallel tenths or sixths, like a descant transposed downward. The low B in bar 1 does not return until the culmination of the refrain, marking the midpoint and end of each stanza and imbuing the second statement of the refrain with a certain leaden finality. For all the numbed regularity of the quaver declamation, one looks at the slur markings in the bass of bars 6–7 and sees the gentle, swinging motion that departs from and returns to the ostinato pitch, moving higher with each swing. The melody is a masterpiece of classical balance in the first half (the dominant-to-tonic pitches are outlined in the first and fourth phrases while the interval C♯–F♯ sounds three times in the interior of the melody), but with the second half, Schubert departs from that perfect symmetry. He seems, as Arnold Feil has pointed out, to have had the second stanza in mind for bars 14–18 ('Das Wild, das ich jage, das ist der Tod, die Heide, die heiß ich die Liebesnot') when he composed the telling extension of the word 'Liebesnot', thus producing a five-bar phrase. The sustained pitch on the accented initial syllable of '*Lie* - besnot', the bright -ie sounds rendering it all the more piercing, is furthermore on a pitch (E in the upper register) that has not previously occurred in the vocal line at all and is dissonant with the continuing F♯ funeral knell (Feil, 75). The occurrence of two large intervallic leaps in succession, an octave leap downwards followed by the leap of a seventh upwards, invests the phrase with a certain energy and dramatic pathos, however muted by the prevailing solemnity. And yet, despite the fact that this second half seems to have been conceived most closely for stanza 2, the lowered or natural seventh degree A♮ that occurs in the vocal line at the beginning of this second half is wonderfully appropriate for the word 'suchen' in stanza 1 as well, all the more because the 'searching' motion is small in scope. The miller does not have far to seek before he finds Death. The A♯ raised seventh degree is reinstated in bar 17 at the word 'Liebesnot', another of the elements that contributes to its powerful effect.

Schubert repeats the words of the refrain each time they occur in order to inflect them differently. The first time, the words 'Mein Schatz hat's Grün so gern' are set to an unprepared tonic *major* harmony, the second time sinking into the lower register on the tonic minor. What we hear first is tragic irony, a bitter twist on the cliché association of major mode with brightness, happiness, cheer. Her happiness, summed up in the word 'gern', is his pain. The second time, all irony is gone. The voice joins the funeral knell in declamation that evokes chanting, and the low bass harmonic foundation returns. The first statement of the refrain shares the disembodied texture of the visionary imaginings that precede it, but with the second statement, grief in the here and now returns. The non-refrain lines, one notices, have feminine endings which Schubert concludes at mid-bar, while the refrain has a masculine ending on the word 'gern', placed on the downbeat and prolonged each time. The word paradoxically signifies tragedy for the protagonist, and Schubert's miller dwells on the paradox.

17. Die böse Farbe – Ziemlich geschwind, 2/4, B major–minor

The titles and tonalities announce from the start that these songs are a study in extreme contrasts. Every aspect of 'Die liebe Farbe' is bent to the consistency requisite for a funeral dirge. Its accompaniment and vocal line are both bound to the unceasing ostinato pitch; the figuration never changes character; and the sad solemnity never gives way to another emotional affect, but 'Die böse Farbe' is a masterpiece of seeming disjunction. The succession of frantic, futile desires couched in the subjunctive impel a variety of rhythmic and melodic patterns but always return at the end of each even-numbered stanza to the same cry of pain first heard in bars 19–22 – surely one of Schubert's most wrenching instances of the Neapolitan sixth en route to cadence. There is, one notices, only minimal instrumental breathing room between stanzas, or transition from one shade of emotional desperation to the next. The miller is buffeted by his feelings, and the musical structure reflects the swift succession of changing mental events, from the initial desperate impulse to flee through near-madness to the lyrical recovery of resolution at the end.

The contrasts to come are announced in the introduction, split into *piano*/major-mode arpeggiated harmonies and *forte*/parallel minor/ hammered chordal planes, two bars each (the contrasting phrases to follow are mostly four bars in length). The first half prefigures the accompaniment to the lyrical passages, when the miller is sufficiently collected to sing, and the second foreshadows the subsequent outbreaks of desperation. Both, though, share a similar mid-bar rhythmic accent and the placement of the highest pitches in each half of the bar on the offbeat, one of the indices of extreme tension in this song. The melody pitches B–F♯–C♯–F♯–B in bars 3–4 are a rearrangement of the same perfect intervals in the initial vocal phrase of 'Die liebe Farbe', the first indication that elements from the preceding song will now be used to express the opposite of their original connotations.

Schubert reverses the contrasting planes – now *forte* first, *piano* second – in the setting of stanza 1, actually the first half of a section that ends with the cadence on B in bars 21–2. The fierce energy of the miller's desire to escape is evident in the vocal line that vaults upwards a tenth (the vocal line exactly duplicates the span of the right-hand part in bars 1–2) and the resolute symmetry of the harmonic rhythm, two-bar phrases, and diatonic harmonies: this is the subjunctive converted, for a brief time, by Schubert's music into the future tense as certainty ('I *will* go forth into the world …'). Resolve is quickly defeated by the omnipresent green, the accompanimental pattern now weakened and deprived of its bass octave doubling in the consequent phrase (bars 9–12). The vocal line sinking down by degrees in bars 9–10, the dotted rhythms (these come from bar 6) and therefore the slight durational emphases on the words 'nur … grün … grün … wär'', and the dominant minor harmonies are the indices of a sudden depressive turn, after which the miller as suddenly reverts in bars 12–16 to the energetic resolve of the first phrase. The actions of fleeing the scene, of stripping green leaves from the trees, are followed each time by grief in the parallel minor. But with the direct mention of death at the end of stanza 2, the symmetry of the contrasting planes is shockingly over-thrown, not on the initial 'toten-' ('deathly') of this compound word but on the final 'bleich' ('pale'). In Schubert's reading, the miller realizes a split second after he sings 'toten-' that he is actually contemplating his own death. The shock sends him reeling and the music jolting upwards in a massive deceptive motion (bar 20), all the more so for the offbeat arrival on the Neapolitan sixth and the high G♮ in the vocal part (the brighter, more open sound of the diphthong -ei after the closed, darker vowels of 'toten-' adds to the effect). In a different context, '-bleich' would not receive such emphasis, but Schubert makes us hear the moment of revelation the instant it happens. The two-bar cadence so violently thrown off course must then be restated to conclude on B, and one notices that it is sung and played *forte*. Now there is an action that *is* possible for him, lying in wait behind the impossibility of bleaching all the green leaves with his tears.

Whenever the miller speaks as if to someone else, to the colour green or the miller maid, the melodic writing becomes less lyrical and more decla-matory – he 'sings' his despair to himself and 'speaks' to the destructive forces that have shattered his life. In Schubert's setting of stanza 3 ('Ach Grün, du böse Farbe du'), the moment of fateful realization in bars 19–20 echoes and re-echoes throughout bars 23–6: the motive consisting of sequential descending thirds in the outer voices of the accompaniment comes from the topmost voice of the piano at bar 19. Perhaps because the miller in stanza 3 speaks to the beloved/evil colour, Schubert brings back recognizable elements from 'Die liebe Farbe' – the semiquaver ostinato pitches in the inner voice, the outer voices of the piano part doubled in tenths – but the effect is entirely different, one of driven obsession rather than funereal solemnity. One remembers the hammered triplet semiquavers in Schubert's Op. 1, 'Erlkönig', the pulsations thrumming in the air and inducing a kind of panic-stricken claustrophobia, crowding out breath and rationality together. Schubert reinforces the words 'So stolz, so keck, so schadenfroh', each item in the masochistic catalogue punctuated with a gasping breath, when he has the piano double the voice, the singer leaping down from the ostinato pitch F♯ to join the piano on the offbeat – ingenious emphasis.

In the fourth stanza, Schubert returns to the lyrical breadth of the beginning, especially appropriate for the prolonged farewell the miller imagines singing to the maiden. The action he envisages is all of a piece, and the stanza is entirely lyrical – until 'the little word Farewell' brings back the thunderbolt of bars 19–20. Death and farewell to the beloved/to life are one and the same. The nearness of death and thoughts of the hunter, metonymically and musically invoked by the sound of the hunting horns on the F♯ already associated with death from 'Die liebe Farbe', then impel a brush with the outer fringes of insanity. Both the horn-calls and the text declamation are unnaturally rapid, with two lines of Müller's verse compressed into two bars of music. In each of the phrases of stanza 4 (bars 43–4, 46–7) declamation on the repeated pitch F♯ becomes the point of departure for a frantic vault upwards in the second half of the phrase. With the directive 'O binde von der Stirn dir ab das grüne, grüne Band', insanity's claws dig deeper; the hunting horns are banished, and the harmonic rhythm is suddenly, shockingly, quicker. With each vocal phrase of this ten-bar section, the upper limit presses higher, rising from E to F♯ to G♮ in a musical graph of rising tension.

Schubert's miller recovers his lyrical balance for the final two lines of the stanza. In stanza 4, he has imagined singing farewell to her, and now he does so to a repetition (with slight prosodic variations) of the fourth stanza. The end of the texted body of the song is elided with a literal repetition of the piano introduction as postlude: more than classical container for the formal structure, this recurrence signifies that the contrasts regnant in this song are as forceful at the end as at the beginning.

18. Trock'ne Blumen – Ziemlich langsam, 2/4, E minor–major

For the first time in the cycle, we hear the key of 'Des Baches Wiegenlied', a tritone away from the optimistic vitality of 'Das Wandern' in Bb major. The resemblance between the E minor chords at the start of 'Trock'ne Blumen' – the most minimal of introductions – and the equally chilled beginning of 'Auf dem Flusse', the seventh song of *Winterreise*, must strike anyone familiar with both Schubert–Müller cycles. Here, the chords are as austere as possible, and they mark what is actually a division of each 2/4 bar into halves in 2/8 (Feil, 78). The second beat is not a weaker beat but a strong downbeat, especially apparent when Schubert has the voice rise to the tonic pitch E in the higher register at 'mid-bar' or places an accent on the chromatically-tinged verb 'legen', again at mid-bar. The G major – G minor chords (the Bb of the G minor chords is subsequently respelled as A♯ in the Italian sixth chords at bars 14–15, 28–9) and the cadences on G major are a miniature foreshadowing of the tonal contrasts in the next song. For the austerity of Müller's lines, the page filled with eloquent emptiness, Schubert substitutes a non-stop Dead March in which stanzas 1–3, then stanzas 4–6 are set as two successive musical strophes. The miller, as if in a dulled trance, keeps going, slowly and without stopping until the end of the musical strophe, with only minimal time for breath between phrases; there are no indicated rests in the vocal line until bar 15. Each two-bar phrase in bars 3–10 wavers weakly back and forth between the E minor on which it begins and the G minor on which it ends – Schubert avoids the dominant altogether until bars 11–15, the dotted rhythms a foreshadowing of the triumphal E major resurrection to come. The powerful effect of the half-cadences at the end of each musical strophe (bars 14–15, 28–9) is due in part to the ascent into the upper register, surpassing the upper limits on E for the first time. The bass even ascends an octave higher for the cadential echo in the piano. When Schubert repeats the music of stanzas 1–3 for stanzas 4–6, one notices that among the few variants for prosodic or expressive reasons is a demisemiquaver figure animating still further the verb 'to be' in the line 'und Winter *wird* gehn', underscoring the future tense even on the offbeat. And the half-cadence at the end of the E minor section is melodically altered, the rising-questioning inflection changed so that the apex pitch F♯ sounds on the downbeat of bar 28 at the word 'sie' – 'that *she* gave to me'.

In Schubert's conception, the wonderfully expressive emphasis on 'sie' impels the vision of resurrection that follows, in which the soft funeral drumtaps are succeeded by burgeoning motion. The most striking aspects of the vision of resurrection include the following:

1. The mediant motion between E minor and G major harmonies in the first half now becomes motion a minor third distant in the opposite direction, and the verbs 'wandelt', 'denkt'' and 'meint'' are thus given a harmonic marker to underscore their significance. The brief emphasis on C♯ minor produces melodically the diminished fourth interval that underscores the verb 'meint'' (E–B♯).

2. The diminished seventh harmonies in bars 35–6, 44–5 bring back the G♮s and the A♯–B bass figures from the first half.

3. Not until the miller proclaims, 'Der Mai ist kommen, der Winter ist *aus*' do we hear tonic closure on E in the voice as well as the piano.

Stanzas 7 and 8 consume almost as much musical space as the six preceding, the repetitions tantamount to desperate insistence. 'It *shall*, it *must* be so', the miller asserts, more loudly each time, but because this is fantasy, the illusion dies shortly after the words cease. Schubert vividly traces the dispelling of hope in the postlude. At the start, the piano once again repeats the resurrection figures at the original pitch level, but then sinks an octave lower back into E minor – depression and darkness made audible. Here at the end, Schubert cancels the implicit 2/8 metre by means of a legato slur throughout almost every bar of the postlude. The pulse slows, and all vitality drains away.

19. Der Müller und der Bach – Mäßig, 3/8, G minor–major–minor

The miller is so exhausted by grief and hopelessness that he wavers to and fro. From the beginning, the lute chords of the introduction – the resemblance between the introductions of 'Trock'ne Blumen' and 'Der Müller und der Bach' is hardly coincidental – stagger, their short–long, short–long pattern the preparation for a singer who wobbles even more. When Schubert transgresses prosodic accuracy as often as he does in setting the miller's death-haunted words of stanzas 1–3, it is in order to enact emotions in the text that would credibly warp declamation. The initial word 'Wo' is prolonged beyond its due, the normally weak second syllable of 'Her-ze' is also prolonged, the entire word 'Herze' sways, the miller alternates between stress on the first beat and stress on the second beat, the poetic clause 'Wo ein treues Herze in Liebe vergeht' is divided by a rhythmic/melodic caesura in the middle, the melismatic setting of the adjective 'jedem' rises and falls in an aimless fashion, and so on. The song is slightly but tellingly distorted by the nearness of death and the torpor of extreme grief. Even the ascent to the high F♯ at the word '*Lie* - be' in bar 5, heightened all the more by the acute soprano–bass dissonance, is followed by an immediate exhausted falling-away. A tritone outline in the next phrase culminates in the Neapolitan sixth harmonization of the word 'Lilien', its funerary associations underscored in the darkness of the chord.

Müller has the brook respond to the miller's death-haunted depression with the same poetic construction but transformed, turned around to show the Janus face of life and hope. Schubert does likewise: his brook takes over the miniature ABA form of the miller's music, the durational emphases on the second beat, and many of the same melodic hallmarks but rendered soothing and stable. The brook, for example, easily ascends to the high G that the miller cannot reach; while the miller is too dispirited to do more than circle weakly around the tonic chord, without purposeful motion to any other tonal goal, the brook confidently asserts the dominant pole in the middle of its song. When the brook sings of 'Liebe', it is diatonic and without dissonance, borne aloft on the lyrical ascending sixth associated earlier in the cycle with love's ardour, while the rocking motion in the bass is both consistent and a rhythmic double much of the time for the second-beat stresses in the voice. There are no hidden currents, no concealed disturbances in the placid flow of the right-hand part; everything about the brook's song tells of clarity, symmetry, stability.

The youth, however, is beyond persuasion. The brook continues its soothing undercurrent in the piano, but the lad hears it in the darkened parallel minor and with the resumption of his enfeebled, staggering melodic motion. He wants only to be 'da unten'; overcome by that longing, he gives all music back to the brook in the brook's own major mode – 'So singe nur zu!' – and falls silent after only two stanzas of poetry, not three as in the previous sections. It is left to the brook to 'sing on' in the postlude, the unspoken final stanza of the text, and its song at the end sinks 'da unten' to depths lower than anywhere else in 'Der Müller und der Bach'.

20. Des Baches Wiegenlied – Mäßig, alla breve, E major

Lullabies depend by definition on soothing regularities, especially rhythmic regularity, and on compositional restriction. Too much novelty to engage the mind, and rest will not come. In the 'Schlaflied', D. 527 (to a text by his friend Johann Mayrhofer) and the 'Wiegenlied', D. 498 (poet unknown), Schubert had already shown his affinity for the conventions of cradle songs – rocking motion, moderate or moderately slow tempi, major mode, regular two-beat pulsations, strophic setting, lulling repetition of figures, subtle variations to allay monotony – and he would do so again after *Die schöne Müllerin* in his setting of Johann Gabriel Seidl's 'Wiegenlied', D. 867. But 'Des Baches Wiegenlied' has more on its mind than rest, even rest in death, and Schubert, without abandoning a single convention of the genre, turns them to epiphanic ends.

The lullaby-elegy sounds in the tonality of love's prophesied fulfilment in 'Trock'ne Blumen'. Schubert evidently composed the repeated musical stanza to Müller's first verse; neither prosody nor poetic meaning are as perfectly served in the other four stanzas. Even the motive of a rising scalewise third (the 'lapping' motion) in the introduction and throughout the song echoes the opening words 'Gute Ruh', gute Ruh'' over and over again. Throughout much of the stanza, with the significant exception of bars 16–20, Schubert sounds a funeral knell in the soprano and bass, most often a perfect fifth; he would later use similar means in the piano accompaniment to 'Das Zügenglöcklein', D. 871 (the title refers to a small bell formerly rung in Austrian churches when a parishioner was dying). Between this gentle drone, the two inner voices move together, the voice-exchange between the alto and tenor another form of the chimes that ring softly throughout 'Des Baches Wiegenlied'. The lapping motion by which the alto voice leads from the tonic pitch on the upbeat to the third of the tonic chord on the downbeats, doubled by the voice a third above in bar 5, is in part responsible for the floating sensation Schubert creates, by a minor miracle, in tandem with a bass that bespeaks rootedness and stability. There is no tonic closure in the vocal line until the end of the stanza, and even there, it occurs in mid-bar, not on the first beat, and the final interlude/postlude ends with the fifth of the chord still sounding in the soprano. In places such as the prolonged subdominant harmony of bars 11–15 ('Die Treu ist hier, sollst liegen bei mir'), the singer's avoidance of the root A colours the words with a marked yearning quality. Even before the expansion into the infinite at the poem's end, the music points upwards.

The line 'Wandrer, du müder, du bist zu Haus' is, in Feil's words, the key that unlocks the entire song (Feil, 82). Schubert, however, allows a hint of doubt in the surety of celestial homecoming to peer through the promises of infinite peace. Following Müller's lead, Schubert shifts to trochaic/downbeat rhythms in the vocal line for the first time at those words and ascends to high E on the downbeat for bar 10 (E only appears on the offbeat in the previous phrases) to emphasize the verb in the present tense and therefore the brook's fervent assurances: 'Wanderer, tired one, you *are* at home'. The fervour seems required to allay doubts that the words are

true. The harmonies move away from the repeated patterns of the introduction, and the musical events of bars 10–11, surely devised with stanza 1
in mind, must be counted among the most poignant details of the stanza.
The words 'Wandrer, du müder, du bist zu Haus' – the only words that are
not repeated in this stanza – culminate in a half-cadence on the dominant
of C♯ minor, but the piano in bar 11 refuses the darker atmosphere of
minor mode and moves instead to the subdominant, the plagal relationship
and the brightness of the major an implicit rejection of the relative minor.
In the sombre submediant is awareness of the tragedy that has brought this
wanderer to this house, and the brook-piano will have none of it. Schubert
makes the aspect of denial, of suppressed disturbance, evident when he
overturns the previous phrase structure and does not repeat the two-bar
phrase, instead interjecting a single bar of harmonic preparation in the
piano (bar 11) before the two-bar symmetries resume. The singer then
takes the high E on the downbeat of bar 10 ('du *bist*') and repeats it over
and over ('Die *Treu* is *hier*, sollst *lie* - gen bei mir') but in the brighter
context of major chords, the vocal line now floating high above the piano.

At the end, the brook promises the youth its loving care until time is no
more. Schubert registers the solemnity of the vow and its cosmic breadth –
the ocean of eternity in stanza 1, the sweep of the heavens in stanza 5 –
when he replaces the string quartet texture for the piano with the fullest,
richest chords to be found anywhere in the cycle. He was perhaps
additionally inspired by the last half of stanza 2 ('Heran, heran, / Was
wiegen kann, /Woget und wieget den Knaben mir ein'), as the chordal
figures rock gently back and forth; the swaying motion does not come to
rest on root-position tonic until the final syllable of text. In these neighbour-
note figures, the C♯ minor rejected in bar 11 returns and so do the B♯ s of
bar 10, respelled as C in bar 19, a single outline of a diminished fourth
interval, with its connotations of lamenting. Again, the chromatic incursion
only lasts an instant before diatonic tranquillity is restored, but the tinge of
melancholy thereafter darkens even the expansion into the infinite as the
elegy and the cycle come to an end.

Notes

1 The poet of 'Die schöne Müllerin'

1 Heinrich Kreissle von Hellborn, *Franz Schubert* (Vienna: Carl Gerold's Sohn, 1865), 315–16, and Otto Erich Deutsch, ed., *Schubert: Memoirs by his Friends* (London: Adam & Charles Black, 1958), 200 (hereafter *Memoirs*). Müller's *Siebenundsiebzig Gedichte aus den hinterlassenen Papieren eines reisenden Waldhornisten* were published in October of 1820 (but dated 1821) in the poet's native Dessau by the firm of Christian G. Ackermann. *Die schöne Müllerin* is the first work to appear in the volume on pp. 1–50.

2 See also Albert B. Bach, *The Art Ballad: Loewe and Schubert* (London: W. Blackwood, 1890), 103–9.

3 Wilhelm Müller's *Gedichte aus den hinterlassenen Papieren eines reisenden Waldhornisten II: Lieder des Lebens und der Liebe* (Dessau: Christian G. Ackermann, 1824), dedicated to 'the master of German song', includes Müller's masterpiece, *Die Winterreise*.

4 Heinrich Heine, *Briefe*, ed. Friedrich Hirth (3 vols., Mainz: F. Kupferberg, 1950), vol. I, 269–70. In this letter from 1826, Heine writes, 'with the exception of Goethe, there is no lyric poet whom I admire as much as you'.

5 Henry Wadsworth Longfellow, *Hyperion: A Romance* (Philadelphia, n.d.), book 2, ch. 7, 'Mill Wheels and Other Wheels', 120–2.

6 The fastidious Mendelssohn also turned Zedlitz down, but Carl Loewe obliged with one of his most popular ballads.

7 See Cecilia C. Baumann, *Wilhelm Müller, The Poet of the Schubert Song Cycles: His Life and Works* (University Park, Pa.: The Pennsylvania State University Press, 1981). See also Bruno Hake, *Wilhelm Müller: Sein Leben und Dichten, Kapitel IV: 'Die schöne Müllerin'* (Berlin: Mayer und Müller, 1908).

8 See Max Friedländer, 'Die Entstehung der Müllerlieder: Eine Erinnerung an Frau von Olfers' in *Deutsche Rundschau*, 19/2 (1892), 301–17, and Friedländer, *Die schöne Müllerin: Ein Zyklus von Liedern gedichtet von Wilhelm Müller in Musik gesetzt von Franz Schubert* (Leipzig: C. F. Peters, 1922), 'Introduction', 7–28. Hedwig married Ignaz von Olfers, later the director of the Königliche Museen in Berlin. An important source of information about the *Liederspiel* and its players, about Berlin cultural life at the time, is Marie von Olfers's documentary biography of her ancestor, *Hedwig von Olfers, geb. von Staegemann: Erblüht in der Romantik, gereift in selbstloser Liebe: Aus Briefen zusammengestellt* (2 vols., Berlin: Ernst Siegfried Mittler & Sohn, 1914), the tale of the *Liederspiel*, vol. II, 1–4.

9 *Diary and Letters of Wilhelm Müller*, 38 and 19–20.

10 See Johann Friedrich Reichardt, 'Abhandlung: Etwas über das Liederspiel' in *Allgemeine musikalische Zeitung*, 3/43 (July 1801), cols. 709–17 and Luise Eitel Peake, 'The Song Cycle: A Preliminary Inquiry into the Beginnings of the Romantic Song Cycle and the Nature of an Art Form', Ph.D. dissertation, Columbia University, 1968, ch. 4, 177–91.

11 Johann Friedrich Reichardt, *Goethe's Lieder, Oden, Balladen und Romanzen*, part 3: *Balladen und Romanzen* (Leipzig: Breitkopf & Härtel, 1809); facsimile edn Wiesbaden: Breitkopf &

Härtel, 1969). According to Margarete von Olfers, in *Elisabeth v. Staegemann: Lebensbild einer deutschen Frau 1761–1835* (Leipzig: Koehler & Amelang, 1937), 47–51, Reichardt admired the beautiful and musically gifted Elisabeth, who sang and acted the role of Rose in Reichardt's *Liederspiel Lieb' und Treue* (Love and Fidelity).

12 Achim von Arnim and Clemens Brentano, *Des Knaben Wunderhorn: Alte deutsche Lieder* (Munich: Winkler, 1957, after the original edn: Heidelberg: Mohr und Zimmer, 1806–8), 303–4. Brahms later set this poem in 1868 as Op. 48, no. 2.

13 See Joseph von Eichendorff, *Werke*, ed. Hartwig Schultz (6 vols., Frankfurt: Deutscher Klassiker Verlag, 1987), vol. I: *Gedichte, Versepen*, 84; Clemens Brentano, *Gesammelte Schriften*, ed. Christian Brentano (9 vols., Bern: Herbert Lang, 1970), vol. II, 433; and Justinus Kerner, *Kerners Werke*, ed. Raimund Piffin (6 vols., Berlin & Leipzig: Deutsches Verlagshaus Bong & Co., reprinted Hildesheim & New York: Georg Olms Verlag, 1974), vol. III: *Reiseschatten, Dramatische Dichtungen*, 70–1.

14 Friedrich Rückert, *Rückerts Werke*, ed. Edgar Gross and Elsa Hertzer (8 vols., Berlin & Leipzig: Deutsches Verlagshaus Bong & Co., n.d.), vol. II: *Liebesfrühling*, 164–5. Heinrich Marschner later set this poem as 'An die schöne Müllerin', Op. 106, no. 6.

15 Clemens Brentano's *Gesammelte Briefe von 1795 bis 1842*, vol. VIII of the *Gesammelte Schriften* (Frankfurt: J. D. Sauerländer, 1855), 216.

16 See the author's 'Behind the Scenes: *Die schöne Müllerin* before Schubert', *19th-Century Music* 15/1 (Summer 1991), 3–22.

17 Ludwig Rellstab, *Ludwig Berger: ein Denkmal* (2 vols., Berlin: T. Trautwein, 1846), vol. II, 111–12. Rellstab devotes an entire chapter, albeit a brief one, subtitled 'A late blossom of love – its demise', to Berger's courtship of Luise, whom he delicately does not name. See Dieter Siebenkäs, *Ludwig Berger: Sein Leben und seine Werke unter besonderer Berücksichtigung seines Liedschaffens* (Berlin: Verlag Merseburger, 1963), 19.

18 *Diary and Letters of Wilhelm Müller*, 89.

19 *Ibid.*, 6.

20 Heinrich Lohre, *Wilhelm Müller als Kritiker und Erzähler: Ein Lebensbild mit Briefen an E. A. Brockhaus und anderen Schriftstücken* (Leipzig: F. A. Brockhaus, 1927), letter of 19 February 1827, 274.

21 The memoirs of the writer Karl Förster include an account of the summer afternoon in Dresden when Müller read both *Die schöne Müllerin* and another cycle, *Johannes und Esther*, to his friends and 'Tieck said many encouraging words to him'. See Luise Förster, ed., *Biographische und literarische Skizzen aus dem Leben und der Zeit Karl Försters* (Dresden: Gottschalck, 1846), 171, and Baumann, *Wilhelm Müller*, 46–7.

22 *Diary and Letters of Wilhelm Müller*, 5.

23 Carl Koch, *Bernhard Klein (1793–1832): Sein Leben und seine Werke* (Leipzig: Oscar Brandstetter, 1902), 34–5, also Otto Erich Deutsch, *Schubert: A Documentary Biography*, trans. Eric Blom (London: J. M. Dent & Sons Ltd, 1946; reprinted New York: Da Capo Press, 1977), 436–7, hereafter referred to as *Documents*, and Baumann, *Wilhelm Müller*, 60.

2 Schubert and the genesis of the music

1 Eric Sams, 'Schubert's Illness Re-examined', *The Musical Times* 121 (1980), 15–22, shows that the course of Schubert's illness as traced in the extant documents matches the usual etiology and treatment for syphilis at the time. There was no distinction between the various venereal diseases until after Schubert's death, and therefore a definitive diagnosis is not possible.

2 See Maynard Solomon, 'Schubert and the Peacocks of Benvenuto Cellini' in *19th-Century Music* 12/3 (Spring 1989), 193–206. 'Peacocks' are Cellini's encoded reference to young boys as sexual partners, such being the preference, so Solomon believes, of Schubert and his circle of close friends.

3 *Documents*, 270.

4 On the death of Victor Graf Wimpffen, the manuscript was given to the Gesellschaft der Musikfreunde, in accordance with the directions in a codicil to the will. A facsimile of fo. 1r of the manuscript (bars 1–17) is printed in Franz Schubert, *Neue Ausgabe sämtlicher Werke*, series IV: Lieder, vol. II/a, ed. Walther Dürr (Kassel & Basel: Bärenreiter Verlag, 1975), xxviii. A facsimile of the entire manuscript (two single folios stitched together, the verso side of fo. 2 blank) was included in the 'Anhang' to Max Friedländer's 1922 Peters edition of this cycle.

A list and description of all the major sources is given in Walther Dürr's typescript critical notes for the cycle, more extensive than could be printed in the *Neue Schubert–Ausgabe*. I am grateful to Professor Dürr for sending me a copy of his notes and graciously permitting me to cite information from them.

5 The reminiscence comes from a family chronicle written sometime before 1876, and Hartmann's memory could perhaps be faulty.

6 John Reed, *The Schubert Song Companion* (Manchester: Manchester University Press, 1985), 180.

7 Heinrich Kreissle von Hellborn, *Franz Schubert* (Vienna: Carl Gerold's Sohn, 1865), 142–3.

8 In the same letter (363), Schubert writes, 'It is no longer that happy time during which each object seems to us to be surrounded by youthful radiance, but a period of fateful recognition of miserable reality, which I endeavour to beautify as far as possible by my imagination (thank God)'. In the letter of 31 March 1824 to Leopold Kupelwieser (*ibid.*, 339), Schubert characterizes Leidesdorf as 'truly thoughtful and good' but 'hugely melancholy'. It is no wonder, as Leidesdorf may also have contracted syphilis, the first symptoms manifesting themselves that year.

9 Copies of all or part of the cycle can be found in such important Schubert sources as the Witteczek–Spaun collection, the Spaun–Cornaro Liederalbum, and the Franziska Tremier songbook, as well as others. Walther Dürr believes that the copies of 'Die liebe Farbe', 'Die böse Farbe', and 'Trock'ne Blumen' in the Spaun–Cornaro Liederalbum may be based on a vanished *erste Niederschrift*, or a first stage of the compositional history. The nineteenth-century arrangements include a version of 'Das Wandern' for orchestra, arranged by Ferdinand Schubert in his *Cyclus beliebter Compositionen Franz Schuberts*, now in the Taussig collection of the Lund University Library; an arrangement of 'Der Neugierige' for soprano and orchestra by Franz von Suppé (Gesellschaft der Musikfreunde IV/39289); and an undated nineteenth-century edition of the complete cycle arranged for piano, four hands: *Schöne Müllerin, Winterreise, Schwanengesang und 22 berühmte Lieder von Franz Schubert zu 4 Händen arrangirt von Hugo Ulrich* (Leipzig: C. F. Peters, n.d.).

10 Max Friedländer, in *Schubert–Album Supplement: Varianten und Revisionsbericht zum ersten Bande der Lieder von Franz Schubert* (Leipzig: Peters, 1884), 8ff, stated that the manuscript was in the possession of 'Baron Kutschera, Fünfhaus bei Wien'. According to Kreissle von Hellborn, *Franz Schubert*, 138, Schönstein had given the manuscript to Countess Karoline Esterházy; her aunt, the Countess Rosa von Almasy, then gave it to the singer Julius Stockhausen. In a letter to Heinrich von Herzogenberg of 24 February 1886, Brahms remembered that the Countess Wilhelmine von Wickenburg-Almasy owned 'several transposed miller songs' by Schubert (see *Johannes Brahms im Briefwechsel mit Heinrich und Elisabet von Herzogenberg*, ed. Max Kalbeck (2 vols., Berlin, 1907–8), vol. II, 120), but he seems to have been mistaken. From Baron Kutschera, the manuscript passed to a Herr Kleyle, according to a note in Otto Erich Deutsch's handwritten copy of the 'Revisionsbericht' of the old *Gesamtausgabe*, and was subsequently lost.

11 Franz Schubert, *Die schöne Müllerin* / ein Cyclus von Liedern / gedichtet von Wilh. Müller / in Musik gesetzt / für eine Singstimme mit Pianoforte Begleitung / und dem Hn. Carl Freyherrn von Schönstein gewidmet. Wien, bei Ant. Diabelli & Comp., Graben No. 1133.

12 See Andreas Liess, *Johann Michael Vogl, Hofoperist und Schubertsänger* (Graz & Cologne: Hermann Böhlhaus, 1954). Liess discusses Vogl's association with Schubert and his circle on pp. 60–92 and the singer's interpretations of Schubert's songs on pp. 129–42.

13 Copies of 'Trock'ne Blumen', 'Der Müller und der Bach', 'Des Baches Wiegenlied', and 'Die liebe Farbe', all transposed to lower keys for mezzo-soprano or contralto voice, in the Franziska Tremier Songbook (Vienna City Library, MH 9136) also reflect Vogl's embellishments and alterations. The collection belonged to Franziska or 'Fanni' von Pratobevera von Wiesborn, who married Josef Tremier in 1829; no one presently knows what connection there might be between the Tremier manuscript and Vogl, although it is possible that the Pratobeveras, who were among Schubert's most ardent fans, could have hosted a musical soirée at which Vogl sang and that Fanni and her future husband could have met the great singer then.

14 Robert Schollum, 'Die Diabelli–Ausgabe der "Schönen Müllerin"' in *Zur Aufführungspraxis der Werke Franz Schuberts*, ed. Roswitha Karpf (Munich & Salzburg: Musikverlag Emil Katzbichler, 1981), 140–61

15 In Franz Schubert, *Neue Ausgabe sämtlicher Werke*, series IV; Lieder, vol. II/b, ed. Walther Dürr (Kassel & Basel: Bärenreiter Verlag, 1975), 273–91, Dürr has printed 'Mein!', 'Mit dem grünen Lautenbande', 'Trock'ne Blumen', and 'Der Müller und der Bach' in their entirety as they appear in the Diabelli edition.

16 See Selmar Bagge, 'Der Streit über Schubert's Müllerlieder' in the Leipzig *Allgemeine Musikalische Zeitung* 3/5 (29 January 1868), 36–7. Bagge reproduces an entire newspaper article entitled 'Fr. Schubert's Müllerlieder in verschiedenen Lesarten' from the *Leipziger Tageblatt* (for 3 January 1868; the unnamed writer in turn cites Schönstein's statement in 1864 that he only used the original edition for his performances of the cycle. August Reissmann, in *Franz Schubert: Sein Leben und seine Werke* (Berlin: J. Guttentag, 1873), 151–61, devotes virtually his entire discussion of *Die schöne Müllerin* to a comparison of the first edition with the 'later editions' (unspecified, but clearly descendants of Diabelli) for the purpose of demonstrating the superiority of the former.

17 The critic, possibly Franz Stoepel, for the Munich *Allgemeine Musik–Zeitung* (*Documents*, 795) writes on 28 July 1828 that cycles are difficult to compose because each song is an individual entity that must 'live its own life' and yet form part of a larger whole.

18 Claudius set, in order: 'Wanderschaft' (he reverts to Müller's title), 'Wohin?', 'Halt!', 'Danksagung an den Bach', 'Des Müllers Blumen', 'Die böse Farbe', 'Trock'ne Blumen', 'Der Müller und der Bach', and 'Des Baches Wiegenlied'. The songs, all strophic, are in the simplest *volkstümlich* idiom, without a trace of Schubert's influence.

19 Eduard Hanslick, *Aus dem Concert-Saal: Kritiken und Schilderungen aus 20 Jahren des Wiener Musiklebens 1848–1868* (Vienna & Leipzig: Wilhelm Braumüller, 1897, 2nd revised edn), 106.

20 In a lively letter to his father, written from Düsseldorf on 16 May 1856, Stockhausen described his stay in Vienna and the reception accorded the cycle. The combination of rainy weather and a programme of special interest to the Viennese assured him a full house (his first concert had been ill-attended, owing to warm weather). See Julia Wirth, *Julius Stockhausen: Der Sänger des deutschen Liedes nach Dokumenten seiner Zeit* (Frankfurt: Englert & Schlosser, 1927), 162–3.

21 Hanslick, *Aus dem Concert–Saal*, 238.

22 See Max Kalbeck, *Johannes Brahms* (4 vols., Berlin: Deutsche Brahms-Gesellschaft, 1912, 3rd revised edn), vol. I: *Zweiter Halbband 1856–1862*, 452, and Julia Wirth, *Julius Stockhausen*, 223 (at the performance in Cologne, an actress named Pauline L'Arronge of the Cologne Stadttheater recited the prologue and the three omitted poems) and 293. Stockhausen may also have been the first to sing Schumann's *Dichterliebe*, Op. 48 in its entirety.

23 I am indebted to the Historisches Museum der Stadt Wien for permission to reproduce these illustrations.

24 Carl Schorske, *Fin-de-siècle Vienna* (New York: Alfred A. Knopf, 1980), 221.

3 Romantic illusions: the poetic texts, nos. 1–12

1 See Madeleine Haefeli-Rasi, *Wilhelm Müller: 'Die schöne Müllerin': Eine Interpretation als Beitrag zum Thema STILWANDEL im Übergang von der Spätromantik zum Realismus* (Zurich: Schippert & Co., 1970).

2 On 16 April 1820, the 'rustic song-play' ('ländliches Liederspiel') 'Rose, die Müllerin,' to a text by Adalbert vom Thale (the pseudonym for a General Karl von Decker) and music by Baron Adolph Lauer von Münchofen, was first performed at the Royal Opera House in Berlin. In this version of the tale, the tragic conclusion of both the Stägemann Liederspiel and Müller's cycle is replaced by a happy ending in which Rose and Liepold, the miller lad, are reunited.

3 How appropriate! The *vidas*, or miniature biographies, of Jaufré Rudel (fl. mid-twelfth century) included in medieval manuscripts make him the epitome of *amor lonhdan*, or 'distant love'. Rudel's love for the Countess of Tripoli culminates in his death in her arms – their first meeting. It is ironic that Müller was actually reading Tristan (but whose version?) in October 1815, during the period of his love for Luise, but found 'many indecencies' in the tale. See *Diary and Letters of Wilhelm Müller*, 22.

4 Alan P. Cottrell, *Wilhelm Müller's Lyrical Song-Cycles: Interpretations and Texts* (Chapel Hill, N.C.: The University of North Carolina Press, 1970), 10.

5 Clemens Brentano, *Sämtliche Werke und Briefe* (8 vols., Frankfurt & Stuttgart: Freie Deutsche Hochstift, 1975), vol. VIII, 50.

6 *Diary and Letters of Wilhelm Müller*, ed. Philip Schuyler Allen and James Taft Hatfield (Chicago, Ill.: The University of Chicago Press, 1903), 28.

7 Haefeli-Rasi, *Wilhelm Müller: Die schöne Müllerin*, 20.

8 Cecilia C. Baumann, *Wilhelm Müller: The Poet of the Schubert Song Cycles: His Life and Works* (University Park, Pa.: The Pennsylvania State University Press,1981), 42.

9 For this later addition to the cycle, Müller may have borrowed images and phrases from an earlier *Wanderlied* of his own composition entitled 'Frühlingsmorgen' or 'Morgen' in different sources. The poet invokes Morning allegorically as the beloved: lines 7–8, 'Blümlein weinten die ganze Nacht, / Weil man dich zu Bett gebracht'; lines 15–18, 'Und sie richten sich empor, / Schütteln ab der Träume Flor. / Wie sie wanken, wie sie beben, / Alle Tränen von den Wangen, / Aus dem Herzen alles Bangen, / Alles froh und Alles frei, / Ob's der erste Welttag sei!' See Müller, *Gedichte: Vollständige kritische Ausgabe*, ed. James Taft Hatfield (Berlin: B. Behr, 1906), 35–6.

10 John Reed, *The Schubert Song Companion* (Manchester: Manchester University Press, 1985), 187.

11 Julia Wirth, *Julius Stockhausen: Der Sänger des deutschen Liedes nach Dokumenten seiner Zeit* (Frankfurt: Englert & Schlosser, 1927), 229.

4 Disillusionment and death: the poetic texts continued

1 John Reed, *The Schubert Song Companion* (Manchester: Manchester University Press, 1985), 189.

5 The music of *Die schöne Müllerin*

1 The autograph manuscript of *Die schöne Müllerin* is lost, but if the autograph of *Winterreise* is any indication, then it may have been the publisher, not Schubert, who designated the work as a 'Liedercyclus' on the title page of the first edition.

2 Richard Capell, *Schubert's Songs* (London: Pan Books, 1973, reprint of 1928 1st edn), 232.

3 In June 1816, Schubert composed 'Gott im Frühlinge' (God in springtime), D. 448, about the contemplative joy of harmony with Nature and with God, in E major. Four years after composing *Die schöne Müllerin*, Schubert would again set a poem in which memory, Nature, the human soul, and Death mingle in another masterpiece in E major, 'Der Lindenbaum' from *Winterreise*.

4 John Reed, *The Schubert Song Companion* (Manchester: Manchester University Press, 1986), 489.

5 Paul Robinson, *Opera & Ideas: From Mozart to Strauss* (Ithaca, N. Y.: Cornell University Press, 1985), 70. 'Thus the strophic form of nearly half the songs in *Die schöne Müllerin* plays an important role in creating our sense of the miller's psychology. Schubert and his miller aren't ashamed to sing the same tune over and over.'

6 Arnold Feil, *Franz Schubert: Die schöne Müllerin; Winterreise*, trans. Ann C. Sherwin (Portland, Oreg.: Amadeus Press, 1988), 50, hereafter, 'Feil'.

7 Edward Cone, 'Schubert's Promissory Note: An Exercise in Musical Hermeneutics' in *Schubert: Critical and Analytical Studies*, ed. Walter Frisch (Lincoln, Neb.: University of Nebraska Press, 1986), 13–30.

8 Alfred Einstein, *Schubert: A Musical Portrait* (New York: W. W. Norton, 1951).

Select bibliography

Editions

1. First edition

DIE SCHÖNE MÜLLERIN / ein / CYCLUS VON LIEDERN / gedichtet von / WILHELM MÜLLER / In Musik gesetzt / für eine Singstimme mit Pianoforte Begleitung / dem / Carl Freyherrn von Schönstein / gewidmet von / FRANZ SCHUBERT / 25 Werk ... [1.: handwritten] Heft / Eigenthum der Verleger. / Wien, Sauer & Leidesdorf.

Schuberts Liederzyklen. Die schöne Müllerin. Winterreise und Schwanengesang. In verkleinerter Nachbildung der Originalausgaben herausgegeben und einbegleitet von Heinrich Kralik. n.d. [facsimile of the first edition of the complete cycle]

2. Second edition

Die schöne Müllerin / ein Cyclus von Liedern / [Vignette of a mill and miller maid] / gedichtet von Wilh. Müller. / In Musik gesetzt / für eine SINGSTIMME mit PIANO-FORTE Begleitung / und dem Hn Carl Freyherrn von Schönstein gewidmet / von / FRANZ SCHUBERT. / No. 3525–29. / 25tes Werk. [handwritten: 1]tes Heft. / Eigenthum der Verleger. / Pr. f [handwritten: 1] C.M. / WIEN, / bei Ant. Diabelli & Comp. / Graben No. 1133

3. Later editions

Die schöne Müllerin. Lieder-Cyclus [gedichtet von Wilhelm Müller. In Musik gesetzt von] Franz Schubert. Für das Pianoforte [und eine Singstimme] übertragen von Carl Reinicke. Wien: Spina (185–?]

Die schöne Müllerin; ein Cyclus von Liedern. Gedichte von W. Müller für eine Singstimme mit Begleitung des Pianoforte. Op. 25. Original-Ausgabe. Leipzig, C. F. Peters [1867?] Pl. no. 4614

Die schöne Müllerin, Lieder-Cyclus für eine Singstimme mit Klavierbegleitung ... Original Ausgabe. Leipzig: C. F. Peters [1869?]

Schubert-Album. Supplement. Varianten und Revisionsbericht zum ersten Bande der Lieder von Franz Schubert, ed. Max Friedländer. Leipzig: C. F. Peters, 1884.

Die schöne Müllerin. Ein Zyklus von Liedern gedichtet von Wilhelm Müller. In Musik gesetzt von Franz Schubert, ed. Max Friedländer. Leipzig: C. F. Peters, 1922.

Textual source

Sieben und siebzig / Gedichte / aus den hinterlassenen Papieren / eines / reisenden Waldhornisten. / Herausgegeben / von / Wilhelm Müller. / Dessau, 1821. / Bei Christian Georg Ackermann.

A select list of other composers' settings of poems from 'Die schöne Müllerin'

Berger, Ludwig. *Gesänge aus einem gesellschaftlichen Liederspiele 'Die schöne Müllerin' mit Begleitung des Pianoforte*, Op. 11. Berlin: E. H. G. Christiani [1818].

Claudius, Otto. *Neun Lieder von Wilhelm Müller*. Leipzig: Breitkopf & Härtel, 1833. 'Wanderschaft', 'Wohin?', 'Halt!', 'Danksagung an den Bach', 'Des Müllers Blumen', 'Die böse Farbe', 'Trock'ne Blumen', 'Der Müller und der Bach', 'Des Baches Wiegenlied'.

Curschmann, Carl Friedrich (1800–41). 'Ungeduld', Op. 3, no. 6; 'Danksagung an den Bach', Op. 5, no. 1; 'Mein!', Op. 3, no. 4. Berlin: Schlesinger [184–?]. All three are included in *Curschmann-album. Sammlung der beliebtesten lieder u. terzette mit pianofortebegleitung*. Leipzig, C. F. Peters [1872].

Dorn, Heinrich (1814–92). 'Müllerburschen Abschied. Wandern ist des Müllers Lust', Op. 76, no. 3. Berlin: Schlesinger, [n.d.].

Klein, Bernhard (1793–1832). 'Trock'ne Blumen' from the *Lieder und Gesänge*, no. 5. Berlin: E. H. G. Christiani, [1822].

Marschner, Heinrich (1795–1861). 'Wanderschaft', 'Morgengruß', 'Des Baches Wiegenlied', Op. 63, nos. 1–3. Berlin: Hofmeister.

Reissiger, Carl Gottlieb (1798–1859). 'Der Neugierige', Op. 53, no. 3; 'Des Müllerburschen Halt! und Danksagung an den Bach', Op. 76, no. 1 and 'Die liebe Farbe', Op. 76, no. 3 from *Sechs deutsche Lieder u. Gesänge für eine Tenor- oder Sopran-Stimme mit begleitung des Piano-Forte*. Op. 76. Bonn: N. Simrock [183–].

Spohr, Louis (1784–1859). 'Ungeduld', Op. 94, no. 4 from the *Sechs deutsche Lieder* for alto or baritone and piano. Bonn: N. Simrock, 1837. Reprinted in Louis Spohr, *The Complete Lieder Sets*, ed. Clive Brown (New York & London: Garland Publishing, Inc., 1988), 89–91.

Stark, Ludwig. *Nachtrag zu Franz Schuberts Liedercyklus 'Die schöne Müllerin'*. 'Mühlenleben', 'Erster Schmerz, letzter Scherz', 'Blümlein Vergissmein' von Wilhelm Müller, mit einem Anhang: 'Der traurige Jäger' von Josef von Eichendorff, Op. 54. Stuttgart: Th. Stürmer, circa 1880.

Stern, Julius (1820–83). 'Das Wandern' in *Deutsche Gesänge für eine Singstimme mit Begleitung des Pianoforte*, Op. 13, no. 5. Berlin: Bote & Bock, [185–?]

Taubert, Wilhelm (1811–91). 'Wo ein treues Herze' in *Sechs deutsche Lieder*, Op. 6, no. 2 (Berlin: Trautwein [185–?]); 'Des Müllers Blumen' in *Sechs Lieder mit Begleitung des Pianoforte* (Leipzig: Hofmeister, [185–?]), Op. 22, no. 5; 'Morgengruß', Op. 174, no. 5

Wustrow, A. F. 'Wohin?' and 'Danksagung an den Bach' from the *Neun Gesänge*, Op. 15, nos. 4 and 5. Berlin: Moritz Westphal, [183–?].

Zöllner, Carl Friedrich (1800–60). *Des Müllers Lust und Leid, 6 Gesänge aus dem Liedercyclus 'Die schöne Müllerin' von Wilhelm Müller für vier Männerstimmen*, Op. 6. Leipzig: Fiedlein, 1844.

Secondary literature

Abeken, Hedwig. *Hedwig von Olfers geb. von Staegemann: Ein Lebenslauf*. 2 vols. Berlin: Mittler & Sohn, 1908.

Bagge, Selmar. 'Der Streit über Schubert's Müllerlieder'. Leipzig *Allgemeine Musikalische Zeitung*, 3/2 (29 January 1868), 36–7.

Baumann, Cecilia C. *Wilhelm Müller, The Poet of the Schubert Song Cycles: His Life and Works*. University Park, Pa.: The Pennsylvania State University Press, 1981.

Budde, Elmar. '"Die schöne Müllerin" in Berlin' in *Preussen, Dein Spree-Athen: Beiträge zu Literatur, Theater und Musik in Berlin*, ed. Hellmut Kühn, pp. 162–72. Berlin: Rowohlt, 1981.

Cottrell, Alan P. *Wilhelm Müller's Lyrical Song-Cycles: Interpretations and Texts*. Chapel Hill, N.C.: The University of North Carolina Press, 1970.

Deutsch, Otto Erich. 'Das Urbild der "Schönen Müllerin" (Dichtung und Wahrheit)' in *Jahresbericht des Schubertbundes in Wien über das zweiundfünfzigste Vereinsjahr*, 27–43. Vienna: Verlag des Schubertbundes, 1915.

Schubert: A Documentary Biography, trans. Eric Blom. New York: Da Capo Press, 1977.

Schubert: Memoirs by his Friends. London: Adam & Charles Black, 1958.

Dürr, Walter. '"Manier" und "Veränderung" in Kompositionen Franz Schuberts' in *Zur Aufführungspraxis der Werke Franz Schuberts*, ed. Roswitha Karpf, 124–39. Munich & Salzburg: Musikverlag Emil Katzbichler, 1981.

'Schubert and Johann Michael Vogl: A Reappraisal' in *19th-Century Music* 3/2 (November 1979), 126–40.

Feil, Arnold. *Franz Schubert: Die schöne Müllerin; Winterreise*. With an essay, 'Wilhelm Müller und die Romantik' by Rolf Vollmann. Stuttgart: Philipp Reclam jun., 1975. Trans. Ann C. Sherwin as *Franz Schubert: Die schöne Müllerin; Winterreise*. Portland, Oreg.: Amadeus, 1988.

Friedländer, Max. 'Die Entstehung der Müllerlieder: Eine Erinnerung an Frau von Olfers' in *Deutsche Rundschau* 73 (1892–93), 301–7.

Georgiades, Thrasybulos G. *Schubert: Musik und Lyrik*. Göttingen: Vandenhoeck & Ruprecht, 1967.

Haefeli-Rasi, Madeleine. *Wilhelm Müller: 'Die schöne Müllerin': Eine Interpretation als Beitrag zum Thema STILWANDEL im Übergang von der Spätromantik zum Realismus*. Zurich: Schippert & Co., 1970.

Hake, Bruno. *Wilhelm Müller: Sein Leben und Dichten, Kapitel IV: Die schöne Müllerin*. Berlin: Mayer & Müller, 1908.

Hanslick, Eduard. *Aus dem Concert-Saal: Kritiken und Schilderungen aus 20 Jahren des Wiener Musiklebens 1848–1868*, 71–3, 106–10, and 236–8. Vienna & Leipzig: Wilhelm Braumüller, 1897.

Heuss, Alfred. 'Franz Schuberts und Friedrich Zöllners "Das Wandern ist des Müllers Lust"' in *Zeitschrift für Musik* 96 (1929), 5–10 and 65–70.

Just, Klaus Günther. 'Wilhelm Müllers Liederzyklen "Die schöne Müllerin" und "Die Winterreise"' in *Zeitschrift für deutsche Philologie* 83 (1964), 452–71. Reprinted in *Übergänge: Probleme und Gestalten der Literatur*. Bern & Munich: Francke, 1966, 133–52.

Kramer, Lawrence. 'The Schubert Lied: Romantic Form and Romantic Consciousness' in *Schubert: Critical and Analytical Studies*, ed. Walter Frisch, 200–36. Lincoln, Nebr.: University of Nebraska Press, 1986.

Kreutzer, Hans Joachim. 'Schubert und die literarische Situation seiner Zeit' in *Franz Schubert: Jahre der Kreise 1818–1823: Arnold Feil zum 60. Geburtstag am 2. Oktober 1985*, ed. Werner Aderhold, Walther Dürr and Walburga Litschauer, 29–38. Kassel & Basel: Bärenreiter, 1985.

Müller, Wilhelm. *Diary and Letters of Wilhelm Müller*, ed. Philip Schuyler Allen and James Taft Hatfield. Chicago Ill.: The University of Chicago Press, 1903.

Peake, Luise Eitel. 'The Song Cycle: A Preliminary Inquiry into the Beginnings of the Romantic Song Cycle'. Ph.D. dissertation, Columbia University, 1968.

Reed, John. '*Die schöne Müllerin* reconsidered'. *Music & Letters* 59 (October 1978) 411–17.

Rellstab, Ludwig. *Ludwig Berger, ein Denkmal*. Berlin: T. Trautwein, 1846.

Sams, Eric. 'Schubert's Illness Re-examined' in *The Musical Times* 121 (1980), 15–22.

Schollum, Robert. 'Die Diabelli-Ausgabe der "Schönen Müllerin"' in *Zur Aufführungspraxis der Werke Franz Schuberts*, ed. Roswitha Karpf, 140–61. Munich & Salzburg: Musikverlag Emil Katzbichler, 1981.

Schulze, Joachim. '"O Bächlein meiner Liebe": Zu einem unheimlichen Motiv bei Eichendorff und Wilhelm Müller' in *Poetica: Zeitschrift für Sprach- und Literaturwissenschaft*, 4/2 (April 1971), 215–23.

Solomon, Maynard. 'Franz Schubert and the Peacocks of Benvenuto Cellini' in *19th-Century Music* 12/3 (Spring 1989), 193–206.

Spiecker, Frank. *Luise Hensel als Dichterin: Eine psychologische Studie ihres Werdens auf Grund des handschriftlichen Nachlasses*. Freiburg im Breisgau: Herder & Co., 1936.

Wirth, Julia, ed. *Julius Stockhausen, der Sänger des deutschen Liedes, nach Dokumenten seiner Zeit dargestellt von Julia Wirth, geb. Stockhausen*. Frankfurt: Englert & Schlosser, 1927.

Youens, Susan. 'Behind the Scenes: *Die schöne Müllerin* before Schubert' in *19th-Century Music* 15/1 (Summer 1991), 3–22.

Index

Index

problems with the censors, 4
works (in alphabetical order): 'Das
schönste Lied', 9; *Die Bundesblüthen*,
4; *Frühlingskranz aus dem Plauenschen
Grunde bei Dresden*, 4;
'Frühlingsmorgen', 116; *Gedichte aus
den hinterlassenen Papieren eines
reisenden Waldhornisten*, vols. I and II
(*Waldhornisten-Gedichte*), 1, 3, 4, 9,
10, 31, 42, 112; *Tafellieder für
Liedertafeln*, 4; *Die Winterreise*, 4, 7,
31, 35, 42, 47, 51, 112
Munch, Edvard, 63

Paisiello, Giovanni
*L'amor contrastato, o sia La bella
molinara*, 6

Randhartinger, Benedikt, 1, 22
Reed, John, 14, 50, 57
Reichardt, Johann Friedrich, 5, 6, 19,
112
Rellstab, Ludwig, 7, 8, 113
Roller, Alfred, 28, 30
Rückert, Friedrich, 7, 91, 113
Rudel, Jaufré, 33, 116

Sams, Eric, 13
Schober, Franz von, 12, 14, 16
Schollum, Robert, 19
Schönstein, Karl Freiherr von, 2, 14–15,
17, 72, 114, 115
Schorske, Carl, 30
Schubert, Ferdinand, 15, 17, 20
Schubert, Franz, life
illness, 12–13, 113, 114
Schubert, Franz, works (in alphabetical
order by title)
Alfonso und Estrella, D. 732, 1, 13
'An Schwager Kronos', D. 369, 98
'Auf der Donau', D. 558, 99
'Das Zügenglöcklein', D. 871, 110
'Erlkönig', D. 328, 76, 106
Fierabras, D. 796, 14

'Gott im Frühlinge', D. 448, 116
'Ihr Bild', D. 957, no. 9
(*Schwanengesang*), 95
'Schlaflied', D. 527, 109
'Wiegenlied', D. 498, 109
'Wiegenlied', D. 867, 110
Winterreise, D. 911, 3, 16, 22, 26, 72,
116: 'Auf dem Flusse', 107; 'Der
Leiermann', 102; 'Der
Lindenbaum', 22, 83, 116; 'Der
Wegweiser', 93, 102; 'Die Post', 91;
'Frühlingstraum', 87; 'Gute Nacht',
102; 'Mut', 101
'Wonne der Wehmut', D. 260, 93
Schumann, Robert, 17
Liederkreis, Op. 39, 27
'Widmung', Op. 25, no. 1, 91
Schwind, Moritz von, 14, 15
Seidl, Johann Gabriel, 2, 110
Solomon, Maynard, 12
Sonnleithner, Leopold von, 15, 20
Spaun, Josef von, 14, 16
Spenser, Edmund
'Colin Clouts come home again', 44–5
Spina, Carl Anton, 22, 26
Spohr, Louis, 11
Stägemann, Friedrich August von and
Elisabeth, 4, 113
Stägemann, Hedwig, 4, 7, 112
Stockhausen Julius, 26–7, 52, 114,
115
Széchényi of Sárvár-Felsö-Vidék,
Count Louis, 1

Tieck, Ludwig, 10, 33

Vogl, Johann Michael, 14, 15, 18, 19–22,
72, 115

Weber, Carl Maria von, 1, 11
Wolf, Hugo, 17
'Gesegnet sei das Grün und wer es
trägt' (from the *Italienisches
Liederbuch*), 56